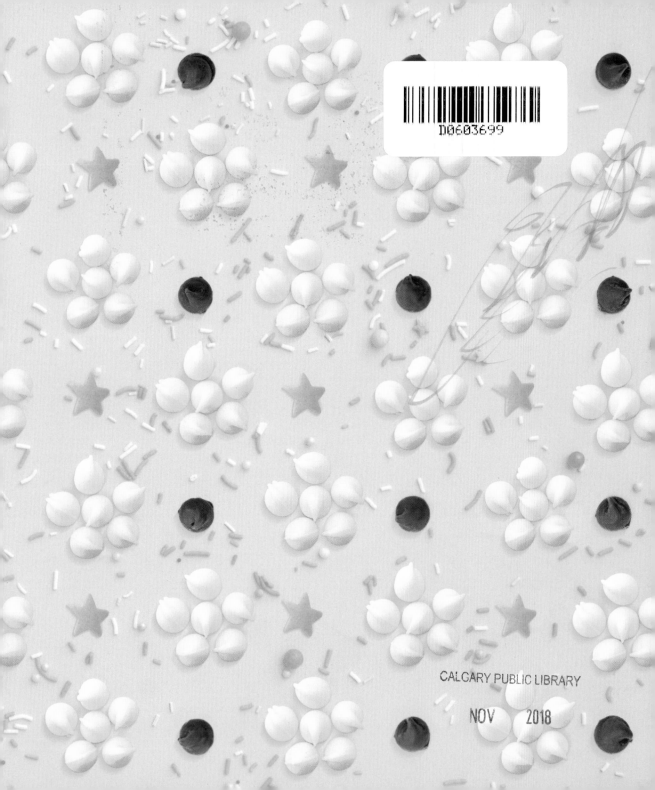
D0603699

CALGARY PUBLIC LIBRARY

NOV   2018

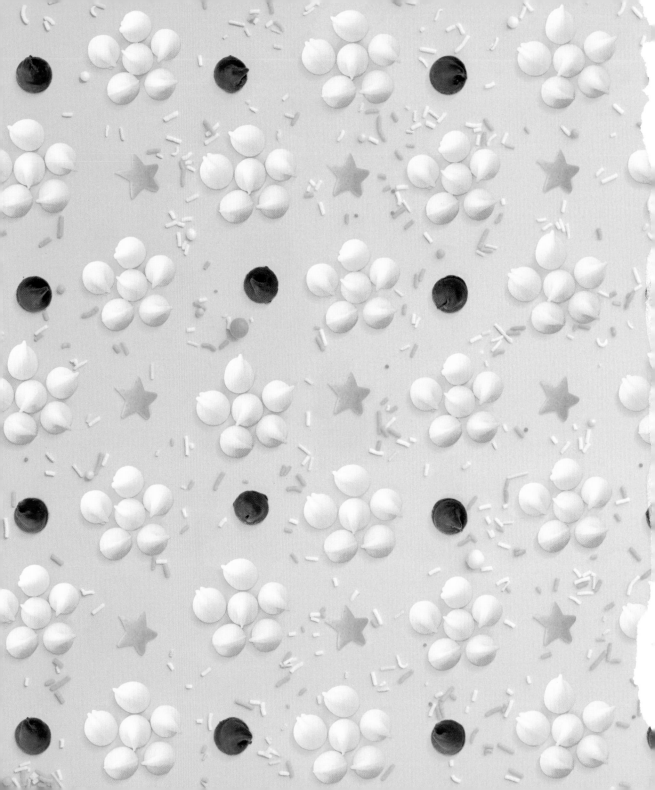

American Girl®

Cookies

Photography **Nicole Hill Gerulat**

weldon**owen**

Contents

Special & Seasonal Cookies

Brownies & Bars

Cookie Fun for Everyone!

Crispy, chewy, or ooey-gooey, we love cookies! Not only do they fill your kitchen with the best aromas ever, but they are super fun to bake—and decorate. Invite friends over after school or on the weekend to have a cookie party. Choose a few of your favorite recipes, bake them together, and then divide and conquer the decorations. Everyone's creativity will shine through, and you can all swap cookies at the end of the party.

All good cookies start with good dough, so be sure to check out our tips for making, shaping, and baking on pages 9–10. The right tools are key—you don't need many, but it's important to have a few essentials on hand before you get started. Decorating is the fun stuff! Throughout this book, we give oodles of ideas, but use your imagination. There are endless combos of sprinkles, sanding sugar, edible beads, stars, and even flowers to play with.

From classics, such as Mini Chewy Chocolate Chip Cookies (page 17) or Snickerdoodles (page 30), to sugar cookies (an entire chapter is dedicated to them!), to super-rich brownies and bars, we have a recipe for everyone. Whatever your style—whether you're daring, playful, colorful, or classic—baking is a great way to create mouthwatering goodies with your own special flair. And last but not least, don't forget a big glass of milk!

Tip-top baking tips

★

★ When making dough, turn off the electric mixer periodically to scrape down the bowl with a rubber spatula in between adding ingredients. This will help the ingredients to combine better.

★ If dough is too hard to roll directly from the fridge, let it stand at room temperature for a few minutes before rolling. You can also use your hands to mold the dough into a ball if it starts to crumble.

★ Dust your rolling pin with flour before rolling out dough.

★ To roll dough scraps, gently gather the scraps and press them together with your hands, then roll them out and cut out additional shapes. After a second rolling, discard any remaining dough.

★ Use a metal spatula to transfer cookie dough shapes from your work surface to cookie sheets, and also to transfer hot cookies from cookie sheets to wire cooling racks.

★ When a recipe indicates that a cookie is done when it's "firm to the touch," be careful when touching hot cookies or ask an adult to help.

★ Most cookies can be stored in between layers of parchment paper in an airtight container for up to 3 days. If they have a filling, be sure to store them in the refrigerator.

The tools you'll need

★ **Cookie cutters** come in all shapes and sizes. All-time favorites are butterflies, stars, flowers, and hearts, but use any you like.

★ **Cookie sheets**, especially thick, heavy ones, help cookies bake evenly.

★ **Small metal icing spatulas** are good for spreading icing on cookies and transferring hot cookies to a wire rack to cool.

★ **A piping bag** fitted with a pastry tip is another way to ice cookies and also to pipe cookie dough onto cookie sheets.

★ **A rubber spatula** is helpful for mixing batters and scraping them into pans.

★ **An electric mixer** makes quick work of batters and frostings, and beating egg whites.

★ **Measuring cups and spoons** help you measure ingredients accurately and easily. Choose graduated sets for dry ingredients and a liquid pitcher for wet ingredients.

★ **Oven mitts or pads** protect your hands from hot pans, oven racks, cookie sheets, and baking dishes.

★ **Parchment paper** is paper that has been treated to give it a nonstick surface. It's used to line cookie sheets and baking pans so that baked goods won't stick.

Baking with care

Adults have lots of culinary wisdom, and can help keep you safe in the kitchen. Always have an adult assist you, especially if your recipe involves high heat, hot ovens, sharp objects, and electric appliances.

This symbol appears throughout the book to remind you that you'll need an adult to help you with all or part of the recipe. Ask for help before continuing.

There are lots
of ideas in the pages
ahead, so choose your
favorite and get
started. All you need
is a big batch of
creativity!

Classic
Cookies Galore

Mini Chewy Chocolate Chip Cookies

These smaller versions of everyone's favorite cookie are exactly what you expect them to be: soft, chewy, and studded with chocolate chip goodness. Make sure not to crowd the dough on the baking sheets, as the cookies will spread a little as they bake.

MAKES ABOUT 54 COOKIES

1¼ cups all-purpose flour

1 teaspoon baking soda

½ teaspoon salt

½ cup (1 stick) unsalted butter, at room temperature

½ cup firmly packed light brown sugar

6 tablespoons granulated sugar

1 large egg

1 teaspoon vanilla extract

1 cup mini semisweet chocolate chips

In a medium bowl, whisk together the flour, baking soda, and salt. In a large bowl, using an electric mixer, beat the butter, brown sugar, and granulated sugar on medium speed until well blended, about 2 minutes. Add the egg and vanilla and beat on low speed until well combined. Turn off the mixer and scrape down the bowl with a rubber spatula. Add about half of the flour mixture and mix on low speed just until blended. Add the rest of the flour mixture and mix again just until blended. Turn off the mixer, add the chocolate chips, and stir with a wooden spoon until the chips are mixed evenly into the dough. Cover the bowl with plastic wrap and refrigerate until the dough is firm, about 30 minutes.

Preheat the oven to 350°F. Line 2 cookie sheets with parchment paper.

Drop heaping teaspoons of the dough onto the prepared cookie sheets, spacing the mounds about 2 inches apart. Bake 1 cookie sheet at a time until the edges of the cookies are light golden brown, about 8 minutes. Remove the sheet from the oven and set it on a wire rack. Let cool for 5 minutes, then use a metal spatula to move the cookies directly to the rack. Repeat to bake the rest of the cookies. Let cool completely and serve.

Triple-Chocolate-Chunk Cookies

Packed with chunks of dark, milk, and white chocolate, these cookies are a triple threat. If you like, you can use ⅔ cup each of semisweet, milk chocolate, and white chocolate chips instead of chopping chocolate blocks.

MAKES ABOUT 32 COOKIES

2 cups all-purpose flour

1 teaspoon baking soda

½ teaspoon salt

1 cup (2 sticks) unsalted butter, at room temperature

¾ cup firmly packed light brown sugar

¾ cup granulated sugar

2 large eggs

2 teaspoons vanilla extract

4 ounces (about ⅔ cup) semisweet or bittersweet chocolate, roughly chopped

4 ounces (about ⅔ cup) milk chocolate, roughly chopped

4 ounces (about ⅔ cup) white chocolate, roughly chopped

 Preheat the oven to 350°F. Line 2 cookie sheets with parchment paper.

In a medium bowl, whisk together the flour, baking soda, and salt. In a large bowl, using an electric mixer, beat the butter, brown sugar, and granulated sugar on medium speed until well blended, about 2 minutes. Add the eggs and vanilla and beat on low speed until well combined. Turn off the mixer and scrape down the bowl with a rubber spatula. Add about half of the flour mixture and mix on low speed just until blended. Add the rest of the flour mixture and mix again just until blended. Turn off the mixer, add the chopped chocolate, and stir with a wooden spoon until the chocolate is evenly mixed into the dough.

Drop heaping tablespoons of the dough onto the prepared cookie sheets, spacing the mounds about 3 inches apart. Bake 1 cookie sheet at a time until the cookies are light golden brown on top, 10 to 12 minutes. Remove the sheet from the oven and set it on a wire rack. Let cool for 5 minutes, then use a metal spatula to move the cookies directly to the rack. Repeat to bake the rest of the cookies. Let cool completely and serve.

Classic Peanut Butter Cookies

You'll have lots of fun shaping this cookie dough with your hands. Peanut butter cookies are always best when they're soft and chewy, so take care not to overbake these treats. Definitely serve these cookies with tall glasses of ice-cold milk.

MAKES ABOUT 36 COOKIES

1⅓ cups all-purpose flour

½ teaspoon baking powder

½ teaspoon baking soda

½ teaspoon salt

½ cup (1 stick)
unsalted butter, melted

½ cup firmly packed
light brown sugar

½ cup granulated sugar

1 cup chunky
peanut butter

1 large egg

1 teaspoon vanilla extract

In a medium bowl, whisk together the flour, baking powder, baking soda, and salt. In a large bowl, using an electric mixer, beat the butter, brown sugar, granulated sugar, peanut butter, egg, and vanilla on medium speed until well blended, about 3 minutes. Turn off the mixer and scrape down the bowl with a rubber spatula. Add the flour mixture and mix on low speed just until combined. Cover the bowl with plastic wrap and refrigerate until the dough is firm, about 2 hours.

Preheat the oven to 350°F. Line 2 cookie sheets with parchment paper.

Lightly moisten your hands with water, pinch off about 1 tablespoon of dough, and roll the dough into a ball between your palms. Place the ball on 1 of the prepared baking sheets. Repeat with the remaining dough, spacing the balls about 2 inches apart.

Dip the tines of a fork in flour, then lightly press the tines into each dough ball to flatten it slightly and create a set of parallel lines in one direction, and then repeat in the other direction to make a crosshatch pattern. Bake 1 cookie sheet at a time until the edges are golden brown, 12 to 15 minutes. Remove the sheet from the oven and set it on a wire rack. Let cool for 5 minutes, then use a metal spatula to move the cookies directly to the rack. Repeat to bake the rest of the cookies. Let cool completely and serve.

Ultimate Chocolate Chunk Cookies

A chewy texture and chunks of chopped chocolate make these cookies the kings—or queens!—of chocolate chip cookies. Surprised by the sea salt for sprinkling? Just a pinch on each cookie really brings out the buttery flavor and chocolaty goodness.

MAKES ABOUT 36 COOKIES

2¼ cups all-purpose flour

1 teaspoon baking soda

1 teaspoon salt

1 cup (2 sticks)
unsalted butter,
at room temperature

⅔ cup firmly packed
light brown sugar

⅔ cup granulated sugar

1 large egg plus
2 large egg yolks

2 teaspoons vanilla extract

12 ounces (about 1 cup)
semisweet chocolate,
roughly chopped

Flaky sea salt,
for sprinkling

 Preheat the oven to 350°F. Line 2 cookie sheets with parchment paper.

In a medium bowl, whisk together the flour, baking soda, and salt. In a large bowl, using an electric mixer, beat the butter, brown sugar, and granulated sugar on medium speed until light and fluffy, about 3 minutes. Add the egg, egg yolks, and vanilla and beat on low speed until combined. Turn off the mixer and scrape down the bowl with a rubber spatula. Add the flour mixture and beat on low speed just until blended. Turn off the mixer, add the chocolate chunks, and stir with a wooden spoon until the chocolate is evenly mixed into the dough.

Drop rounded tablespoons of the dough onto the prepared cookie sheets, spacing the mounds about 1 inch apart. Sprinkle the top of each cookie with a pinch of flaky sea salt. Bake 1 cookie sheet at a time until the cookies are golden brown, 8 to 10 minutes. Remove the sheet from the oven and set it on a wire rack. Let cool for 5 minutes, then use a metal spatula to move the cookies directly to the rack. Repeat to bake the rest of the cookies. Let cool until just barely warm and serve.

Chewy White Chocolate Coconut Cookies

Shredded coconut gives these yummy cookies an extra layer of chewiness. If you'd like to change up the flavor a little, use semisweet or milk chocolate chips in place of the white chocolate chips—or try butterscotch or peanut butter chips.

MAKES ABOUT 20 COOKIES

1⅓ cups all-purpose flour

½ teaspoon baking powder

½ teaspoon baking soda

½ teaspoon salt

½ cup (1 stick) unsalted butter, at room temperature

½ cup firmly packed light brown sugar

½ cup granulated sugar

1 large egg

½ teaspoon vanilla extract

1¼ cups sweetened shredded coconut

½ cup white chocolate chips

Preheat the oven to 325°F. Line 2 cookie sheets with parchment paper.

In a medium bowl, whisk together the flour, baking powder, baking soda, and salt. In a large bowl, using an electric mixer, beat the butter, brown sugar, and granulated sugar on medium speed until light and fluffy, about 3 minutes. Reduce the speed to low, add the egg and vanilla, and beat until combined, about 1 minute. Turn off the mixer and scrape down the bowl with a rubber spatula. Add the flour mixture and beat on low speed just until blended. Turn off the mixer, add the coconut and white chocolate chips, and stir with a wooden spoon until the coconut and chips are evenly mixed into the dough.

Drop rounded tablespoons of the dough onto the prepared cookie sheets, spacing the mounds about 2 inches apart. Bake 1 cookie sheet at a time until the cookies are golden brown, 14 to 16 minutes. Remove the sheet from the oven and set it on a wire rack. Let cool for 5 minutes, then use a metal spatula to move the cookies directly to the rack. Repeat to bake the rest of the cookies. Let cool completely and serve.

Oatmeal-Chocolate Chip Cookies

These oatmeal cookies are studded with lots of chocolate chips that turn gooey with baking. You can swap 2 cups of dried cherries for the chocolate chips or opt for a mix of both. For the right chewiness, use old-fashioned rolled oats, not the quick-cooking kind.

MAKES ABOUT 40 COOKIES

2 cups all-purpose flour

**1½ teaspoons
ground cinnamon**

1 teaspoon baking soda

¾ teaspoon baking powder

½ teaspoon salt

**1 cup (2 sticks)
unsalted butter,
at room temperature**

**1 cup firmly packed
light brown sugar**

1 cup granulated sugar

2 large eggs

2 teaspoons vanilla extract

**2½ cups old-fashioned
rolled oats**

**1 (12-ounce) bag (2 cups)
semisweet chocolate chips**

 Preheat the oven to 350°F. Line 2 cookie sheets with parchment paper.

In a medium bowl, whisk together the flour, cinnamon, baking soda, baking powder, and salt. In a large bowl, using an electric mixer, beat the butter, brown sugar, and granulated sugar on medium speed until well combined, about 2 minutes. Add the eggs and vanilla and beat on low speed until well blended. Turn off the mixer and scrape down the bowl with a rubber spatula. Add about half of the flour mixture and mix on low speed just until blended. Add the remaining flour mixture and mix again just until blended. Turn off the mixer, add the oats and chocolate chips, and stir with a wooden spoon until the oats and chips are evenly mixed into the dough.

Drop heaping tablespoons of the dough onto the prepared cookie sheets, spacing the mounds about 2½ inches apart. Bake 1 sheet at a time until the cookies are golden brown, 11 to 14 minutes. Remove the sheet from the oven and set it on a wire rack. Let cool for 5 minutes, then use a metal spatula to move the cookies directly to the rack. Repeat to bake the rest of the cookies. Let cool completely and serve.

Buttery Vanilla Shortbread Cookies

Rich, buttery shortbread is the perfect cookie for a springtime tea party with your friends. In the summer, serve it alongside a bowl of berry ice cream or lemon sorbet. And in the fall or winter, when it's cold outside, dip it in a cup of hot cocoa.

MAKES 12 COOKIES

1½ cups all-purpose flour

¼ teaspoon salt

1 cup (2 sticks) unsalted butter, at room temperature

¼ cup granulated sugar, plus 1 tablespoon for sprinkling

¼ cup powdered sugar

2 teaspoons vanilla extract

Preheat the oven to 300°F. Have ready a 9-inch square baking pan.

In a small bowl, whisk together the flour and salt. In a large bowl, using an electric mixer, beat the butter on high speed until fluffy and pale yellow, about 3 minutes. Add the the ¼ cup granulated sugar and the powdered sugar and beat on medium speed until well combined. Add the vanilla and beat until well mixed. Turn off the mixer and scrape down the bowl with a rubber spatula. Add the flour mixture and mix on low speed just until blended.

Using the rubber spatula, scrape the dough into the baking pan. Flour your fingers and press the dough into an even layer. Sprinkle the 1 tablespoon granulated sugar evenly over the top. Bake until the edges of the shortbread are golden brown, about 1 hour. Remove the pan from the oven and set it on a wire rack. Immediately use a thin, sharp knife to cut the shortbread in half, then cut each half crosswise into six 1½-inch rectangular bars. While the shortbread is still hot, use a toothpick or wooden skewer to poke holes into the cookies, decorating them with dots. Let cool for 30 minutes, then use an offset spatula to move the cookies directly to the rack. Repeat to bake the rest of the cookies. Let cool completely and serve.

Chocolate-Dipped Butter Cookie Triangles

Invite a few friends over to make these rich, buttery cookies dipped in chocolate and decorated with festive sprinkles. Make sure to let the chocolate set up before serving the cookies, or else be prepared for messy fingers!

MAKES ABOUT 18 COOKIES

2 cups all-purpose flour

½ teaspoon salt

1 cup (2 sticks) unsalted butter, at room temperature

½ cup sugar

2 teaspoons vanilla extract

1 (12-ounce) bag (2 cups) semisweet or bittersweet chocolate chips

Rainbow sprinkles, for decorating

In a medium bowl, whisk together the flour and salt. In a large bowl, using an electric mixer, beat the butter and sugar on medium speed until light and fluffy, about 3 minutes. Add the vanilla and beat until well combined. Turn off the mixer and scrape down the bowl with a rubber spatula. Add the flour mixture and beat on low speed just until blended.

Lightly dust a clean work surface with flour. Using the rubber spatula, scrape the dough out onto the work surface, then shape it into a disk with your hands. Wrap the disk in plastic wrap and refrigerate for 30 minutes.

Preheat the oven to 350°F. Line a cookie sheet with parchment paper.

Dust your work surface with flour and set the dough on the surface. Roll out the dough to ¼-inch thickness. Using a pizza cutter and a ruler, cut the dough into 4-inch squares, then cut each square in half diagonally into triangles. Transfer to the prepared cookie sheet, spacing them about 1½ inches apart. Bake until the edges of the cookies are golden brown, 12 to 14 minutes. Remove the sheet from the oven and set it on a wire rack. Let the cookies cool.

Place the chocolate chips in a medium microwave-safe bowl. Microwave on high power, stirring every 30 seconds, just until the chips are melted and smooth. Dip each cookie halfway into the melted chocolate, then let the excess chocolate drip back into the bowl. Carefully place the cookie back on the cookie sheet and sprinkle the chocolate-coated side with rainbow sprinkles. Let stand at room temperature until the chocolate has set, then serve.

Tasty toppings

Instead of using sprinkles, try topping these cookies with chopped candy canes, toasted nuts, or pretzels.

Snickerdoodles

These cookies with a silly name are seriously scrumptious. They're what happens when balls of sugar cookie dough are rolled in cinnamon-sugar before baking. For extra yumminess, serve these soft and chewy goodies with ice cream or mugs of hot cocoa.

MAKES ABOUT 36 COOKIES

2¾ cups all-purpose flour

1 teaspoon baking powder

¼ teaspoon salt

1 cup (2 sticks) unsalted butter, at room temperature

1¾ cups sugar

2 large eggs

2 teaspoons vanilla extract

1 teaspoon ground cinnamon

 Preheat the oven to 350°F. Line 2 cookie sheets with parchment paper.

In a medium bowl, whisk together the flour, baking powder, and salt. In a large bowl, using an electric mixer, beat the butter and 1½ cups of the sugar on medium speed until well blended, about 1 minute. Add the eggs and vanilla and beat on low speed until combined. Turn off the mixer and scrape down the bowl with a rubber spatula. Add about half of the flour mixture and mix on low speed just until blended. Add the remaining flour mixture and mix again just until blended.

In a small bowl, stir together the remaining ¼ cup sugar and the cinnamon.

Scoop up 1 rounded tablespoon of dough. Scrape the dough off the spoon into your palms and roll the dough into a ball. Drop the ball into the cinnamon-sugar and roll it around to coat it completely. Place the ball on a prepared cookie sheet. Continue scooping, shaping, and rolling the dough in the sugar, spacing the balls about 3 inches apart on the cookie sheets.

Bake 1 cookie sheet at a time until the edges of the cookies are lightly browned but the tops are barely colored, 10 to 12 minutes. Remove the sheet from the oven and set it on a wire rack. Let cool for 5 minutes, then use a metal spatula to move the cookies directly to the rack. Repeat to bake the rest of the cookies. Let cool completely and serve.

Chocolate Brownie Cookies

An ooey-gooey cookie combined with a soft, fudgy brownie?
Yes, please! Serve these easy-to-make sweets with glasses
of cold milk or tucked into bowlfuls of vanilla ice cream.

MAKES ABOUT 36 COOKIES

½ cup all-purpose flour

¼ teaspoon baking powder

¼ teaspoon salt

4 tablespoons
unsalted butter

12 ounces (about 1 cup)
semisweet or bittersweet
chocolate, chopped

¾ cup firmly packed
light brown sugar

2 large eggs

1 teaspoon
vanilla extract

Preheat the oven to 350°F. Line 2 cookie sheets with parchment paper.

In a small bowl, whisk together the flour, baking powder, and salt. In a medium saucepan, combine the butter and chocolate. Set the pan over low heat and stir constantly until the mixture is smooth. Don't let it get too hot! Remove the pan from the heat and let it cool for about 10 minutes.

Add the brown sugar, eggs, and vanilla to the chocolate mixture and whisk until well blended. Stir in the flour mixture until blended. Refrigerate the dough in the saucepan for about 5 minutes.

Drop rounded tablespoons of the dough onto the prepared cookie sheets, spacing the mounds about 1½ inches apart. Bake 1 cookie sheet at a time until the edges of the cookies are set but the centers are still slightly soft, 10 to 12 minutes. Remove the sheet from the oven and set it on a wire rack. Let cool for 5 minutes, then use a metal spatula to move the cookies directly to the rack. Repeat to bake the rest of the cookies. Let cool completely and serve.

Sugar Cookie-Tastic

Sugar Cookie Cutouts

Buttery and crisp, these sugar cookies have a delicate vanilla flavor that makes them delicious on their own, but they are also perfect for decorating. Cut out shapes using your favorite cutters, then give the cookies pizzazz with colorful icings and cute sprinkles.

MAKES ABOUT 30 (3-INCH) COOKIES

3 cups all-purpose flour

1 teaspoon baking powder

½ teaspoon salt

1 cup (2 sticks) unsalted butter, at room temperature

1¼ cups sugar

1 large egg

2 teaspoons vanilla extract

1 tablespoon heavy cream

Royal Icing (page 39) or Vanilla Icing (page 36)

Rainbow sprinkles, sanding sugar, or other decorations of your choice

Step 1: In a medium bowl, whisk together the flour, baking powder, and salt. In a large bowl, using an electric mixer, beat the butter and sugar on medium-high speed until light and fluffy, 2 to 3 minutes. Add the egg and vanilla and beat on low speed until well combined. Turn off the mixer and scrape down the bowl with a rubber spatula. Add the flour mixture in three batches, mixing on low speed after each addition, until the flour is almost blended in. Turn off the mixer and scrape down the bowl again. Add the cream and beat on low speed just until combined.

Step 2: Lightly dust a clean work surface with flour. Using the rubber spatula, scrape the dough out onto the work surface, then use your hands to shape it into a flattened rectangle. Wrap the dough in plastic wrap and refrigerate until firm, at least 1 hour or up to overnight. (The dough can be wrapped in a second layer of plastic wrap and frozen for up to 1 month. Let it thaw overnight in the refrigerator before rolling and baking.)

Preheat the oven to 350°F. Line 2 cookie sheets with parchment paper.

Lightly dust your work surface with flour, unwrap the dough, and set it on the surface. If the dough is too hard to roll directly from the refrigerator, let it stand at room temperature for a few minutes. Dust your rolling pin with flour and roll out the dough to an even ¼-inch thickness.

~ Continued on page 36 ~

Smart cookie

Dip cookie cutters in flour before pressing them into the dough, and place them close together to minimize scraps.

⁓ *Continued from page 35* ⁓

Use your hands to help mold the dough into a ball before rolling if it starts to crumble. Using your choice of cookie cutters, cut out shapes from the dough. With a metal spatula, carefully move the cutouts to the prepared cookie sheets, spacing them about 1 inch apart. Gather the dough scraps and press them together, then roll them out and cut out additional shapes.

Bake 1 cookie sheet at a time until just the edges, not the centers, of the cookies are light golden brown, 14 to 16 minutes. Remove the sheet from the oven and set it on a wire rack. Let cool for 5 minutes, then use the metal spatula to move the cookies directly to the rack. Repeat to bake the rest of the cookies. Let cool completely.

Using icing and sprinkles—and your creativity!—decorate the cookies (see pages 39–40). Let the icing dry at room temperature until firm, at least 6 hours or up to overnight.

Vanilla Icing

In a medium bowl, whisk together 2 cups powdered sugar, 2 tablespoons warm water, 1 tablespoon light corn syrup, and 1 teaspoon vanilla extract until smooth. Add 2–3 dabs of gel paste food coloring, if you like, and whisk to combine. Add more water if icing is too thick.

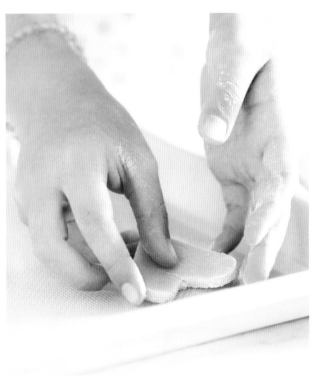

Pipe like a pro

Piping tips for pastry bags come in a variety of shapes and sizes—the smaller the numeral, the smaller the hole.

Royal Icing

This stiff white icing, made by whipping powdered sugar with water and meringue powder, got its name after it was used to ice Queen Victoria's white wedding cake in England in the 1800s. Luckily for us, it's the perfect icing to top sugar cookies, too.

MAKES ABOUT 3 CUPS

4 cups powdered sugar

3 tablespoons meringue powder

½ cup warm water, plus more as needed

½ teaspoon vanilla extract or ¼ teaspoon almond extract (optional)

Gel paste food coloring in your favorite colors (optional)

In a large bowl, using an electric mixer, beat the sugar, meringue powder, ½ cup warm water, and vanilla (if using) on medium speed until the mixture is very thick but drizzleable, 7 to 8 minutes. To test if the consistency is correct, drizzle a spoonful of icing onto itself in the bowl; it should sit on the surface for about 5 seconds. If it is too thick, stir in additional warm water 1 teaspoon at a time with a rubber spatula.

Icing Technique: Flooding If using food coloring, divide the royal icing among small bowls, using one bowl for each color you want to make. Add just a dab or two of food coloring to each bowl and mix well; if needed, stir in more food coloring until the desired color intensity is reached.

To fill a pastry bag, firmly push a ⅛-inch round piping tip (or other desired size) down into the small hole at the bottom of the bag. Form a cuff by folding down the top one-third of the bag. Place one hand under the cuff. Using a rubber spatula, scoop icing into the bag with your other hand, no more than half full. Unfold the cuff, push the icing down toward the tip, and twist the bag closed where the icing ends. Squeeze the bag from the top when you pipe.

Pipe icing around the edge of a cookie to form a border. Using the same or a different color, pipe the icing into the center of the cookie and let it run to the border. Gently tap the cookie against the work surface to get the icing to settle into a smooth, even layer.

~ Continued on page 40 ~

> **Handy helper**
> *Use a large wide-rimmed glass to hold your piping bag while you fill it and to rest it in between decorating.*

~ *Continued from page 39* ~

To create a design on top of the first icing layer, let dry at room temperature until slightly hardened, about 2 hours. Cover and refrigerate the unused icing until needed; stir well before use. Pipe your second design on top, then let dry at room temperature until the icing is firm, at least 6 hours or up to overnight.

Icing Technique: Swirling Place ¼ cup of royal icing into each of 3 small bowls. Add just a dab or two of food coloring to each bowl and mix well; if needed, stir in more food coloring until the desired color intensity is reached. Spoon each colored icing into a pastry bag fitted with a ¼-inch round tip.

Pipe one color of icing around the edge of a cookie to form a border, then pipe icing into the center of the cookie and let it run to the border. Gently tap the cookie a couple of times against the work surface to get the icing to settle into a smooth, even layer.

While the icing is still wet, pipe horizontal parallel lines of one or both of the other colors across the cookie. Lightly drag the tip of a toothpick from top to bottom through the lines. Wipe the toothpick clean, then drag it through the lines in the opposite direction, from the bottom to the top, spaced about ½ inch from the first swirl. Continue dragging the toothpick through the lines, moving in opposite directions and wiping the toothpick clean between each pass. Let the icing dry until firm, at least 6 hours or up to overnight.

Donut Cookies

Super bright and cheery, donut cookies will make everyone's day.
Don't be afraid to use bold icing colors and sprinkles—the crazier the
better! Bake a bunch and invite friends over to help you decorate them.

MAKES ABOUT 40 COOKIES

Dough for Sugar
Cookie Cutouts
(page 35), prepared
through Step 2

Royal Icing (page 39)

Pink and blue gel paste
food coloring, or any
2 to 3 colors of your choice

Rainbow sprinkles,
for decorating

 Preheat the oven to 350°F. Line 2 cookie sheets with parchment paper.

Lightly dust your work surface with flour and set the dough on the surface.
If the dough is too hard to roll directly from the refrigerator, let it stand at
room temperature for a few minutes. Dust your rolling pin with flour and roll
out the dough to ¼-inch thickness. Using a 4-inch donut cutter, cut out rounds
from the dough, then remove the center "hole" from each round. With a metal
spatula, carefully move the cutouts to the prepared cookie sheets, spacing them
about 1 inch apart. Gather the dough scraps and press them together, then roll
them out and cut out additional shapes.

Bake 1 cookie sheet at a time until the edges of the cookies are light golden
brown, about 12 minutes. Remove the sheet from the oven and set it on a wire
rack. Let cool for 5 minutes, then use the metal spatula to move the cookies
directly to the rack. Repeat to bake the rest of the cookies. Let cool completely.

Divide the icing evenly among 3 small bowls. Add a very small amount of pink
food coloring to one bowl, a larger amount of pink food coloring to the second
bowl, and blue food coloring to the third bowl, then mix well; if needed, stir
in more food coloring until the desired color is reached. Using a pastry bag or
small icing spatula, spread icing over a cookie. Gently tap the cookie against the
work surface to get the icing to settle into a smooth, even layer, then decorate
with sprinkles. Repeat to ice and decorate the remaining cookies. Let the icing
dry at room temperature until firm, at least 6 hours or up to overnight.

Chocolate Sugar Cookies

These cookies are what happens when you add cocoa powder to classic sugar cookie dough. The dark color makes it difficult to tell when they're done. After the cookies have baked, gently press the centers with your finger. They should feel firm, not squishy.

MAKES ABOUT 30 (3-INCH) COOKIES

2¼ cups all-purpose flour

⅓ cup unsweetened cocoa powder, sifted

½ teaspoon baking powder

½ teaspoon baking soda

¼ teaspoon salt

¾ cup (1½ sticks) unsalted butter, at room temperature

1 cup firmly packed light brown sugar

¼ cup granulated sugar

1 large egg

1 teaspoon vanilla extract

Royal Icing (page 39) or Vanilla Icing (page 36)

Rainbow sprinkles, sanding sugar, or other decorations of your choice

In a medium bowl, whisk together the flour, cocoa powder, baking powder, baking soda, and salt. In a large bowl, using an electric mixer, beat the butter and sugars on medium-high speed until light and fluffy, 2 to 3 minutes. Add the egg and vanilla and beat on low speed until well combined. Turn off the mixer and scrape down the bowl with a rubber spatula. Add the flour mixture and mix on low speed just until blended. Scrape the dough onto a clean work surface, then shape it into a disk. Wrap in plastic wrap and refrigerate until firm, at least 1 hour or up to overnight.

Preheat the oven to 350°F. Line 2 cookie sheets with parchment paper.

Lightly dust your work surface with flour and set the dough on the surface. Dust your rolling pin with flour and roll out the dough to ¼-inch thickness. Using cookie cutters, cut out shapes from the dough. With a metal spatula, move the cutouts to the prepared cookie sheets, spacing them 1 inch apart. Gather the dough scraps, then roll them out and cut out additional shapes.

Bake 1 cookie sheet at a time until the centers of the cookies are firm to the touch, 12 to 15 minutes. Remove the sheet from the oven and set it on a wire rack. Let cool for 5 minutes, then use the metal spatula to move the cookies directly to the rack. Repeat to bake the rest of the cookies. Let cool completely.

Using icing and sprinkles, decorate the cookies (see pages 39–40). Let the icing dry at room temperature until firm, at least 6 hours or up to overnight.

Jam Swirls

Sweet, sticky jam rolled up in sugar cookie dough makes these treats as pretty as they are tasty. The centers are deliciously soft and chewy, while the outsides are buttery and crisp. If you like, swap out the strawberry jam for your favorite flavor.

MAKES ABOUT 30 COOKIES

Dough for Sugar Cookie Cutouts (page 35), prepared through Step 2

2 cups strawberry jam

Sanding sugar or granulated sugar, for sprinkling

 Preheat the oven to 350°F. Line 2 cookie sheets with parchment paper.

Lightly dust your work surface with flour, and set the dough on the surface. Dust your rolling pin with flour and roll the dough into a 12-by-16-inch rectangle about ¼ inch thick, with the long side facing you. Using an offset spatula, evenly spread 1 cup of the jam over the lower half of the dough, leaving a ½-inch border around the edges. Starting at the bottom edge, tightly roll up the jam-covered dough into a log, stopping when you reach the center.

Carefully flip the dough so that the log is now on the top and the unrolled half of the dough is on the bottom. Evenly spread the remaining 1 cup jam onto the other half of the dough, again leaving a ½-inch border around the edges. Tightly roll up the jam-covered dough into a log as you did the first side, stopping when you reach the center. The two logs should be rolled up in opposite directions and meet in the center. Gently press the two logs together. Using a paring knife, trim the ends to even them off. Carefully move the logs to a cookie sheet and refrigerate or freeze until firm, about 30 minutes.

Using a knife, cut the chilled logs crosswise into ½-inch-thick slices. Place the slices on the prepared cookie sheets, spacing them about 1½ inches apart. Sprinkle each swirl with sugar. Bake 1 cookie sheet at a time until the edges of the cookies are light brown, 14 to 16 minutes. Remove the sheet from the oven and set it on a wire rack. Let cool for 5 minutes, then use a metal spatula to move the cookies directly to the rack. Repeat to bake the rest of the cookies.

Rainbow Cookies

You can create rainbow-like cookies by dividing a batch of sugar cookie dough into thirds and tinting each a different color. For the Fourth of July, try coloring one portion red and another portion blue. Or for Valentine's Day, use three different shades of pink.

MAKES ABOUT 40 COOKIES

Dough for Sugar Cookie Cutouts (page 35), prepared through Step 1

Pink, purple, and turquoise gel paste food coloring, or any 3 colors of your choice

White sanding sugar, for sprinkling

Lightly dust a clean work surface with flour. Scrape the dough out onto the work surface, then divide it into thirds. Add 1 or 2 dabs of pink food coloring to one portion, 1 or 2 dabs of purple food coloring to the second portion, and 1 or 2 dabs of turquoise food coloring to the third portion. Using your hands, knead each piece of dough until it is evenly colored. Wrap each dough in plastic wrap and refrigerate until chilled, about 30 minutes.

Using your hands, shape each portion of dough into a plank measuring 12 inches long, 2 inches wide, and 1 inch tall. Stack the planks on top of each other, placing the purple in the middle. Gently press the stack to seal the layers. Wrap tightly in plastic wrap and refrigerate until firm, about 1 hour.

Preheat the oven to 350°F. Line 2 cookie sheets with parchment paper.

Using a knife, trim the sides of the dough stack to create a rectangular shape. Lightly brush all sides with water and sprinkle evenly with sanding sugar. Cut the dough crosswise into ¼-inch-thick slices. Using a metal spatula, place the slices on the prepared cookie sheets, spacing them about 1 inch apart.

Bake 1 cookie sheet at a time until the centers of the cookies are firm to the touch, 12 to 14 minutes; don't allow them to brown. (Be careful when touching the cookies—they're very hot!) Let cool for 5 minutes, then use the metal spatula to move the cookies directly to the rack. Repeat to bake the rest of the cookies. Let cool completely and serve.

Love Heart Cookies

These adorable hearts are the cookie version of the small pastel-colored Valentine's Day candies stamped with love-inspired messages. Place each cookie in a cellophane bag, tie the bags with red or pink ribbons, and hand them out as Valentine's "cards."

MAKES ABOUT 36 COOKIES

Royal Icing (page 39)

Pink, yellow, blue, and purple gel paste food coloring, or any 4 pastel colors of your choice

Sugar Cookie Cutouts (page 35), cut into 3-inch hearts, baked, and cooled

Edible color marker (optional)

If you will not be using an edible color marker, measure out ¼ cup of the icing and set it aside in an airtight container. Evenly divide the (remaining) icing among 4 small bowls. Add a tiny amount of pink, yellow, blue, and purple food coloring, 1 color per bowl, and mix well; if needed, stir in more food coloring until the desired color intensity is reached. Using a small icing spatula, spread icing onto a cookie. Gently tap the cookie against the work surface a couple of times to get the icing to settle into a smooth, even layer. Repeat to ice the remaining cookies.

Let the icing dry at room temperature until firm, at least 6 hours or up to overnight.

Using an edible color marker, write Valentine-inspired phrases in the middle of each cookie, such as "Be Mine," "I Love You," "xoxo," "BFF," and "QT." Alternatively, spoon the reserved icing into a pastry bag fitted with an ⅛-inch round tip and pipe the phrases onto the cookies. (To store the cookies, layer them between pieces of parchment paper in an airtight container. They will keep for up to 4 days at room temperature.)

Confetti Cookies

With colorful sprinkles both inside and out, every bite of these cookies is like a party. You can change the sprinkles to match the occasion or holiday—use red and green for Christmas; red, white, and blue for the Fourth of July; or pink and red for Valentine's Day.

MAKES ABOUT 36 COOKIES

COOKIES

2¾ cups all-purpose flour

1 teaspoon baking powder

¼ teaspoon salt

1 cup (2 sticks) unsalted butter, at room temperature

1½ cups granulated sugar

2 large eggs

2 teaspoons vanilla extract

2 tablespoons rainbow sprinkles, such as nonpareils

ICING

2½ cups powdered sugar

8 teaspoons whole milk

2 teaspoons vanilla extract

Rainbow sprinkles, for decorating

Preheat the oven to 350°F. Line 2 cookie sheets with parchment paper.

To make the cookies, in a medium bowl, whisk together the flour, baking powder, and salt. In a large bowl, using an electric mixer, beat the butter and granulated sugar on medium speed until well blended, about 1 minute. Add the eggs and vanilla and beat on low speed until well combined. Turn off the mixer and scrape down the bowl with a rubber spatula. Add about half of the flour mixture and mix on low speed just until blended. Add the rest of the flour mixture and mix again just until blended. Turn off the mixer, add the sprinkles, and stir with a wooden spoon until the sprinkles are mixed evenly into the dough.

Scoop up 1 rounded tablespoon of dough. Roll the dough into a ball using your palms, and place on a prepared cookie sheet. Repeat with the remaining dough, spacing the balls about 3 inches apart. Bake 1 cookie sheet at a time until the edges of the cookies are light golden brown, about 13 minutes. Remove the sheet from the oven and set it on a wire rack. Let cool for 5 minutes, then use a metal spatula to move the cookies directly to the rack. Repeat to bake the rest of the cookies. Let cool completely.

To make the icing, in a small bowl, whisk the powdered sugar, milk, and vanilla until smooth. Spoon about 1 tablespoon of the icing onto each cookie, letting it drip over the edges a little. Decorate with rainbow sprinkles. Let the icing dry at room temperature until firm, at least 2 hours.

Stained Glass Cookies

Crushed Jolly Rancher candies sprinkled into dough cutouts melt in the oven and look like panes of colorful stained glass. Make some cookies for eating and some for hanging as ornaments—they're so sparkly and pretty when light shines through them!

MAKES ABOUT 30 (3-INCH) COOKIES

1 (7-ounce) bag Jolly Rancher candies in assorted colors

Dough for Sugar Cookie Cutouts (page 35), prepared through Step 2

 Preheat the oven to 350°F. Line 2 cookie sheets with parchment paper, then lightly grease the parchment with nonstick cooking spray.

Separate the candies by color and place each color in a heavy-duty zipper-lock plastic bag. Seal the bag and use a rolling pin to crush the candies.

Lightly dust your work surface with flour and set the dough on the surface. Dust your rolling pin with flour and roll out the dough to ¼-inch thickness. Using cookie cutters, cut out shapes from the dough. (Large hearts, stars, and flowers work well.) With a metal spatula, carefully move the cutouts to the prepared cookie sheets, spacing them about 1 inch apart. Using smaller cookie cutters, cut out a "window" from each shape and remove the dough from that area. If you plan to hang the cookies like ornaments, use a drinking straw to punch out a hole at the top of each cookie. Gather the dough scraps, then roll them out and cut out additional shapes. Discard any remaining dough. Refrigerate or freeze the cookie sheets until the cutouts are firm, at least 15 minutes.

Bake 1 cookie sheet at a time for about 8 minutes. Remove the sheet from the oven and carefully fill the windows of each cutout with crushed candies. Return to the oven and continue to bake until the edges of the cookies are light brown and the candies have melted, 6 to 8 minutes. Remove the sheet from the oven and set it on a wire rack. Repeat to bake and fill the rest of the cookies. Let the cookies cool completely on the cookie sheets. If you'll be hanging the cookies, thread a piece of ribbon or twine through the hole in each cookie.

Three-Tiered "Cake" Cookies

Packaged in cellophane and tied with pretty ribbons, these cookie stacks are adorable party favors for a birthday celebration. If you like, switch out the food colorings and use ones that match the theme or decorations of your event.

MAKES 25 COOKIES

Dough for Sugar Cookie Cutouts (page 35), prepared through Step 2

Royal Icing (page 39)

Yellow, red, and pink gel paste food coloring

Assorted sanding sugars, for decorating (optional)

25 candy flowers (optional)

Preheat the oven to 350°F. Line 2 cookie sheets with parchment paper.

Have ready 3 round cookie cutters: 2 inches, 1½ inches, and 1 inch. Lightly dust your work surface with flour, unwrap the dough, and set it on the surface. If the dough is too hard to roll directly from the refrigerator, let it stand at room temperature for a few minutes. Dust your rolling pin with flour and roll out the dough to an even ¼-inch thickness. Use your hands to help mold the dough into a ball before rolling if it starts to crumble. Using the cookie cutters, cut out rounds from the dough; you will need 25 of each size. With a metal spatula, carefully move the cutouts to the prepared cookie sheets, grouping like sizes on each cookie sheet and spacing the rounds about 1 inch apart. Gather the dough scraps and press them together, then roll them out and cut out additional rounds. Discard any remaining dough.

Bake 1 cookie sheet at a time until the edges, not the centers, of the cookies are light golden brown, 8 to 10 minutes for the small and medium rounds and 12 to 14 minutes for the large rounds. Remove the sheet from the oven and set it on a wire rack. Let cool for 5 minutes, then use the metal spatula to move the cookies directly to the rack. Repeat to bake the rest of the cookies. Let cool completely.

Measure ¾ cup of the icing into each of 3 small bowls. Add a very small amount of yellow, red, and pink food coloring, one color per bowl, and mix well. (Use the red food coloring to tint the icing dark pink, not red.) If needed, stir in more

Cookies for days

Store cookies in a single layer in an airtight container. They will keep for up to 3 days at room temperature.

food coloring until the color is reached. Spoon each icing into a pastry bag fitted with a ¼-inch round tip (see page 39).

Pipe yellow icing around the edge of a 2-inch cookie to form a border, then pipe icing into the center of the cookie and let it run to the border. Gently tap the cookie against the work surface a couple of times to get the icing to settle into a smooth, even layer. Repeat with the remaining 2-inch cookies. If desired, sprinkle the cookies with sanding sugar.

Ice the remaining cookies the same way, using the light pink icing for the 1½-inch cookies and the dark pink icing for the 1-inch cookies. If desired, sprinkle the cookies with sanding sugar.

Let the icing on the cookies dry at room temperature until firm, at least 6 hours or up to overnight. Cover and refrigerate the remaining icing until you're ready to assemble the cookies; stir vigorously before use.

To assemble the "cakes," pipe a ½-inch dot of icing in the center of each 2-inch cookie, then place a 1½-inch cookie on top. Pipe a ½-inch dot of icing in the center of each 1½-inch cookie, and top with a 1-inch cookie. If using candy flowers, pipe a dot of icing on the bottom of each candy flower and place in the center of each "cake." Pipe decorative pink dots on each tier of each cookie.

Let the assembled cookies dry at room temperature until firm, at least 2 hours.

Galaxy Cookies

Reach for the stars with these super cool cosmic cookies. If you like, use different sizes of star cutters and/or different combinations of food colorings in each bowl for a really colorful starry night!

MAKES ABOUT 40 COOKIES

Sugar Cookie Cutouts (page 35), cut into 3-inch stars, baked, and cooled

Vanilla Icing (page 36)

Pink, blue, and purple gel paste food coloring

Edible glitter and/or edible silver star sprinkles, for decorating (optional)

 Line 2 cookie sheets with parchment paper.

Divide the icing evenly among 3 bowls. Dip a toothpick into the pink food coloring, then dip the coloring into a bowl of icing. Dip a clean toothpick into the blue food coloring, then dip the coloring into same bowl. Do the same with another clean toothpick and the purple food coloring. Then use the toothpick to gently swirl the food colorings into the icing. Don't overswirl or the colors will blend together—be sure to leave a good amount of white icing showing through. Repeat this process with the remaining 2 bowls of icing.

Dip the surface of a cookie into the icing and gently twist it to let any excess icing run off. Place the cookie icing-side-up on 1 of the prepared cookie sheets and sprinkle with edible glitter or stars (if using). Repeat with the remaining cookies. When the first bowl of icing no longer has colored swirls or if the colors have started to blend together too much, use the next bowl of icing.

Let the icing on the cookies dry at room temperature until firm, at least 1 hour or up to overnight. (Store the cookies in an airtight container, layered between sheets of parchment paper. They will keep for 3 days at room temperature.)

Flower Cookies

Nothing says spring like pretty flowers. You can use just one color of icing to decorate your cookies, or make the border and the center two different hues. Or you could pipe individual petals, depending on the shape of your cutter.

MAKES ABOUT 30 (3-INCH) COOKIES

Royal Icing (page 39)

Gel paste food coloring in your favorite color(s) (optional)

Sugar Cookie Cutouts (page 35), cut into 3-inch flower shapes, baked, and cooled

Sanding sugars and/or sprinkles, for decorating (optional)

Edible flowers, such as pansies, nasturtiums, rose petals, mini roses, violets, and geraniums, for decorating (optional)

 If you are using food coloring to tint your icing, divide the icing among small bowls, using one bowl for each color you want to make. Add just a dab or two of one food coloring to each bowl and mix well; if needed, stir in more food coloring until the desired color intensity is reached. Spoon each icing into a pastry bag fitted with a ⅛-inch round tip (see page 39).

Pipe icing around the edge of a cookie to form a border, then pipe icing—the same color or a different one—into the center of the cookie, letting it run to the border. Gently tap the cookie against the work surface a couple of times to get the icing to settle into a smooth, even layer. Sprinkle the cookie with sanding sugar or sprinkles or decorate with edible flowers, if using. Repeat with the remaining cookies and icing.

Let the icing on the cookies dry at room temperature until firm, at least 6 hours or up to overnight. (To store the cookies, layer them between pieces of parchment paper in an airtight container. They will keep for up to 3 days at room temperature.)

Marbled Sugar Cookies

These swirled sweets are easy and super fun to make, but they look so impressive! Choose food coloring to match the occasion or your mood. Try red for Valentine's Day, green for St. Patrick's Day, orange for Halloween, or pastels for Easter or a spring party.

MAKES ABOUT 30 (3-INCH) COOKIES

Sugar Cookie Cutouts (page 35), prepared through Step 1

Gel paste food coloring in your favorite color

Lightly dust a clean work surface with flour. Scrape the dough out onto the work surface, then divide it in half. Add 1 or 2 dabs of food coloring to one half of the dough. Knead the dough until it is evenly colored. Pinch off about 1 tablespoon of colored dough (no need to be exact!) and roll it into a ball between your palms. Repeat until you've shaped all of the colored dough. Wash your hands to remove any food coloring.

Shape the noncolored dough into balls in the same way. Arrange balls in a tightly packed checkerboard pattern, alternating the colored balls with noncolored balls. Gently knead all of the balls together until swirls are visible—be careful not to overknead or the swirls will be lost. Shape the dough into a disk, wrap in plastic wrap, and refrigerate until chilled, 30 to 60 minutes.

Preheat the oven to 350°F. Line 2 cookie sheets with parchment paper.

Lightly dust your work surface with flour and set the dough on the surface. Roll out the dough to ¼-inch thickness. Cut the dough into desired shapes using cookie cutters. Place the cookies on the prepared cookie sheets, spacing them about 1 inch apart. Gather the dough scraps, trying to keep as much of the swirl pattern as you can, then roll and cut out additional shapes. Bake 1 cookie sheet at a time until the centers of the cookies are firm to the touch, about 12 minutes; don't allow them to brown. Remove the sheet from the oven and set it on a wire rack. Let cool for 5 minutes, then use a metal spatula to move the cookies directly to the rack. Repeat to bake the rest of the cookies.

Pretty packages
Colored boxes, patterned tissue paper, cellophane bags, and shiny ribbons are great for wrapping and gifting cookie treats.

Special & Seasonal Cookies

Swirly Meringues

Meringue, or egg whites whipped with sugar until light and airy, can be soft, like the topping on a lemon meringue pie, or they can be crisp like these cool unicorn-looking cookies. Make sure your egg whites have no bits of yolk and that your bowl is clean.

MAKES ABOUT 24 COOKIES

4 large egg whites, at room temperature

1 teaspoon salt

2 cups powdered sugar, sifted

2 teaspoons vanilla extract or 1 teaspoon almond or peppermint extract

Blue and purple gel paste food coloring

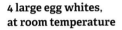 Line 2 cookie sheets with parchment paper. Using a pencil, trace twenty-four 2-inch circles on each sheet of parchment. Remove the parchment from the cookie sheets and lightly spray the sheets with nonstick cooking spray. Turn the parchment over and re-line the cookie sheets; you should be able to see the traced circles through the paper.

In a large clean bowl, using an electric mixer, beat the egg whites on medium-high speed until foamy, about 1 minute. Add the salt. Continue beating on medium-high speed until the whites form a dense foam, about 1 minute. Beating continuously, gradually add the sifted sugar, about 2 tablespoons at a time, then continue to beat until the meringue is glossy and very fluffy, about 15 minutes. Add the vanilla and beat just until combined, about 1 minute.

Fit a large pastry bag with a ½-inch star tip (see page 39). Using a clean paintbrush, paint 1 long vertical stripe of blue food coloring against the right side of the pastry bag, and 1 long vertical stripe against the left side of the bag. Now paint 1 long vertical stripe of purple food coloring against the top of the pastry bag, and 1 long vertical stripe against the bottom side of the bag. Carefully spoon the meringue into the pastry bag using a rubber spatula, trying not to disturb the lines of food coloring; leave about 2 inches free at the top. Gently twist the bag closed.

~ *Continued on page 72* ~

Easy eggs

Separate egg whites and yolks when eggs are cold, but wait to whip the whites until they're at room temperature.

～ *Continued from page 71* ～

Pipe the meringue onto the prepared cookie sheets, starting at the edge of each traced circle, moving the bag in a circular motion and working your way around to the center of the traced circle so that the meringue forms a coil. Refill the piping bag with any remaining meringue, and pipe more circles. (Add more food coloring stripes before adding the remaining meringue, if needed.) Let stand at room temperature, uncovered, for 30 minutes.

Preheat the oven to 250°F.

Bake the meringues 1 cookie sheet at a time until firm and dry to the touch, 25 to 30 minutes, rotating the sheet about halfway through. If they still feel tacky, turn off the oven and leave them in the oven until completely dry. Remove the sheet from the oven and set it on a wire rack. Repeat with the remaining meringues. Let cool completely on the sheet and serve. (To store the cookies, layer them between pieces of parchment paper in an airtight container. They will keep for up to 3 days at room temperature.)

Chill out!

These double-chocolate treats are extra yummy when they're cold, so pop a few in the freezer to snack on anytime.

Chocolate-Covered Mint Wafers

If Girl Scouts Thin Mints are one of your favorite cookies, then you'll love these minty, chocolate-dipped wafers. For deep, dark chocolaty goodness, make sure to use Dutch-process cocoa powder, not natural cocoa powder, in the cookies.

MAKES ABOUT 40 COOKIES

COOKIES

1¼ cups all-purpose flour

¾ cup granulated sugar

¾ cup unsweetened Dutch-process cocoa powder

1 teaspoon baking soda

¼ teaspoon baking powder

½ teaspoon salt

¾ cup (1½ sticks) unsalted butter, at room temperature

1 large egg

1 teaspoon vanilla extract

½ teaspoon peppermint extract

1 tablespoon heavy cream

GLAZE

1¼ pounds semisweet or bittersweet chocolate, finely chopped

½ teaspoon canola oil

½ teaspoon peppermint extract

To make the cookies, in a medium bowl, whisk together the flour, granulated sugar, cocoa powder, baking soda, baking powder, and salt. In a large bowl, using an electric mixer, beat the butter on medium speed until light and fluffy, about 3 minutes. Add the egg and beat on low speed until well blended. Add the flour mixture and beat on low speed until combined, about 2 minutes. Turn off the mixer and scrape down the bowl with a rubber spatula. Add the vanilla and peppermint extracts and the cream. Raise the speed to medium and beat until the dough comes together, about 2 minutes.

Using the rubber spatula, scrape the dough out onto the work surface. Using your hands, form the dough into a disk, wrap it tightly in plastic wrap, and refrigerate until well chilled, about 30 minutes.

Preheat the oven to 375°F. Line 2 cookie sheets with parchment paper.

Dust your work surface lightly with flour, unwrap the dough, and set it on the surface. Dust your rolling pin with flour and roll out the dough to an even ¼-inch thickness. Using a 2½-inch round cookie cutter, cut out rounds from the dough. Using a metal spatula, carefully move the cutouts to the prepared cookie sheets, spacing them about 1 inch apart. Gather the dough scraps and press them together, then roll them out and cut out more rounds. If the dough is too soft and sticky to roll, wrap it in plastic wrap and refrigerate until slightly firm, about 15 minutes.

~ Continued on page 76 ~

Chocolate shortcut

Look for chocolate discs, also called coating wafers, for the minty glaze. They're easy to melt and stir, so they're great for dipping.

〜 *Continued from page 75* 〜

Bake 1 cookie sheet at a time until the centers of the cookies are firm to the touch, 8 to 10 minutes. (Be careful when touching the cookies—they're very hot!) Remove the sheet from the oven and set it on a wire rack. Let cool for 5 minutes, then use a metal spatula to move the cookies directly to the rack. Repeat to bake the remaining cookies. Let cool completely. Reserve the parchment-lined cookie sheets.

To make the glaze, place the chocolate in a medium microwave-safe bowl. Microwave on high power, stirring every 30 seconds, just until the chocolate is melted and smooth. Don't let it get too hot! Stir in the oil and peppermint extract.

Dip each cookie into the glaze and use 2 forks to turn the cookie so that it's coated on both sides. Using the forks, lift out the cookie and gently shake it, allowing excess glaze to fall back into the bowl. Place the glazed cookie back on 1 of the parchment-lined cookie sheets. Repeat with the remaining cookies and glaze. (If the glaze starts to harden, microwave it on high power, stirring every 15 seconds, until it has remelted.) Refrigerate the cookies uncovered until the glaze is set, about 20 minutes. Serve the cookies chilled or at room temperature. (To store the cookies, layer them between pieces of parchment paper in an airtight container. They will keep for up to 3 days in the refrigerator.)

Homemade Oreos

If you don't have a pastry bag for piping the filling onto these iconic sandwich cookies, fill a gallon-size zipper-lock plastic bag halfway with the filling. Push the filling into one corner of the bag, twist the top closed, and snip off about ¼ inch from the corner.

MAKES ABOUT 12 COOKIES

COOKIES

1¼ cups all-purpose flour

¾ cup granulated sugar

¾ cup unsweetened
Dutch-process
cocoa powder

1 teaspoon baking soda

¼ teaspoon baking powder

¼ teaspoon salt

¾ cup (1½ sticks)
unsalted butter,
at room temperature

1 large egg, plus
1 large egg yolk

FILLING

½ cup (1 stick)
unsalted butter,
at room temperature

1½ cups powdered sugar

1 tablespoon whole milk

1 teaspoon vanilla extract

 Preheat the oven to 375°F. Line 2 cookie sheets with parchment paper.

To make the cookies, in a large bowl, whisk together the flour, granulated sugar, cocoa powder, baking soda, baking powder, and salt. Add the butter and, using an electric mixer, beat on low speed for 2 minutes. Add the egg and egg yolk and beat on medium speed until it forms a dough, about 2 minutes.

Dust a clean work surface with flour and roll out the dough to an even ¼-inch thickness. Using a 2-inch round cookie cutter, cut out rounds of the dough. Move them to the prepared cookie sheets, spacing them about 1 inch apart. Gather the dough scraps together, then roll them out and cut out additional rounds. If the dough is too sticky to roll, wrap it in plastic wrap and refrigerate until slightly firm, about 15 minutes. You should have about 24 rounds.

Bake 1 cookie sheet at a time until the centers of the cookies are firm to the touch, 8 to 10 minutes. Remove the sheet from the oven and set it on a wire rack. Let cool for 5 minutes, then move the cookies directly to the rack. Let cool completely.

To make the filling, in a large bowl, combine the butter, powdered sugar, milk, and vanilla. Using an electric mixer, beat on medium-high speed until smooth, about 3 minutes. Scrape the filling into a pastry bag fitted with a ½-inch tip. Turn half of the cookies bottom side up. Pipe about 2 teaspoons of the filling onto each overturned cookie. Top with the remaining cookies, bottom side down, and gently press together so the filling runs just to the edges.

Sugar-and-Spice Star Sandwich Cookies

These yummy stars are made of sugar and spice—and they're filled with fruity jam. For this recipe, you'll need two star-shaped cookie cutters, one that measures about 3 inches and a smaller one that's about 1 to 2 inches.

MAKES ABOUT 24 COOKIES

2¾ cups all-purpose flour

1 teaspoon baking powder

¼ teaspoon baking soda

1 teaspoon ground cinnamon

1 teaspoon ground allspice

¼ teaspoon ground nutmeg

¼ teaspoon salt

¾ cup (1½ sticks) plus 2 tablespoons unsalted butter, at room temperature

1 cup firmly packed dark brown sugar

1 large egg

1 tablespoon molasses

1 tablespoon heavy cream

1 cup strawberry jam (or your favorite flavor)

Powdered sugar, for dusting

In a medium bowl, whisk together the flour, baking powder, baking soda, cinnamon, allspice, nutmeg, and salt. In a large bowl, using an electric mixer, beat the butter and brown sugar on medium-high speed until light and fluffy, 2 to 3 minutes. Add the egg and molasses and beat on low speed until well combined. Add the flour mixture and mix on low speed just until blended. Add the cream and mix on low speed just until combined. Form the dough into a disk, wrap it tightly in plastic wrap, and refrigerate until firm, at least 1 hour or up to overnight.

Preheat the oven to 350°F. Line 2 cookie sheets with parchment paper.

Lightly dust your work surface with flour and set the dough on the surface. Roll out the dough to ¼-inch thickness. Using a 3-inch star-shaped cookie cutter, cut out stars from the dough. Transfer the cutouts to the prepared cookie sheets, spacing them about 1 inch apart. Repeat with any remaining dough scraps. Use a smaller star-shaped cookie cutter to cut out the center from half of the larger stars, then remove the dough from the centers.

Bake 1 cookie sheet at a time until the tips of the cookies are golden brown, 10 to 12 minutes. Remove the sheet from the oven and set it on a wire rack. Let cool for 5 minutes, then move the cookies directly to the rack. Repeat to bake the remaining cookies. Let cool completely. Using a small icing spatula, spread a thin layer of jam on each solid star. Top with the cookies with the centers cut out, dust lightly with powdered sugar, and serve.

Easy rollin'
If the dough is too hard to roll directly from the refrigerator, let it stand at room temperature for a few minutes.

Chocolate Sweetheart Sandwich Cookies

Make sure to slightly underbake the heart-shaped chocolate cookies for these adorable treats. If the cookies are soft, the filling won't squish out when you bite into a sandwich. You can flavor the filling with vanilla or raspberry. If you can't decide, do half and half.

MAKES ABOUT 30 COOKIES

Dough for Chocolate Sugar Cookies (page 46), chilled at least 1 hour

Heart-shaped sprinkles and/or pink and white sanding sugar for decorating (optional)

1 cup (2 sticks) unsalted butter, at room temperature

¾ cup powdered sugar

1½ teaspoons vanilla extract or ¼ cup strained raspberry preserves

Pinch of salt

 Preheat the oven to 350°F. Line 2 cookie sheets with parchment paper.

Lightly dust your work surface with flour and set the dough on the surface. Roll out the dough to ¼-inch thickness. Using a 2-inch heart-shaped cookie cutter, cut the dough into hearts. Transfer the cutouts to the prepared cookie sheets, spacing them 1 inch apart. Repeat with any remaining dough scraps. Sprinkle the cutouts with sanding sugar, if using.

Bake 1 cookie sheet at a time until the cookies are firm to the touch, 10 to 12 minutes. Remove the sheet from the oven and set it on a wire rack. Let cool for 5 minutes, then use the metal spatula to move the cookies directly to the rack. Repeat to bake the rest of the cookies. Let cool completely.

In a large bowl, using an electric mixer, beat the butter and sugar on low speed until combined. Increase the speed to medium-high and beat until light and fluffy, about 3 minutes. Add the vanilla and salt and beat on low speed just until combined. Spoon the mixture into a pastry bag fitted with a ¼-inch round tip (see page 39).

Turn half of the cookies bottom side up. Pipe the butter mixture filling onto each overturned cookie unti it almost reaches the edge. Top with the remaining cookies, bottom side down. Roll the sides of the sandwiches in heart-shaped sprinkles, if using. Refrigerate until the filling is firm, about 1 hour. Serve the cookies chilled or at room temperature.

Chocolate-Filled Vanilla Sandwich Cookies

The dough for these cookies is piped with a pastry bag into rosettes, which is just a fancy word for small flower-like shapes. Make sure the ingredients are at room temperature, so the dough is soft enough to squeeze through the tip of the pastry bag.

MAKES ABOUT 15 COOKIES

2¼ cups all-purpose flour

½ teaspoon salt

¾ cup (1½ sticks) plus 2 tablespoons unsalted butter, at room temperature

1 cup powdered sugar

1 large egg

1 teaspoon vanilla extract

Chocolate Glaze (page 89), chilled

Preheat the oven to 325°F. Grease 2 cookie sheets with nonstick cooking spray and line them with parchment paper.

In a medium bowl, whisk together the flour and salt. In a large bowl, using an electric mixer, beat the ¾ cup butter and sugar on medium-high speed until light and fluffy, 2 to 3 minutes. Add the egg and vanilla and beat on low speed until combined. Add the flour mixture and mix on low speed just until blended. Scrape the dough to a pastry bag fitted with a ¾-inch open star tip (see page 39).

Using firm pressure and a circular motion, pipe 1¼-inch rosettes onto the prepared cookie sheets, spacing them about 1 inch apart. Refrigerate or freeze the cookie sheets until the dough is firm, about 15 minutes.

Bake 1 cookie sheet at a time until the cookies are firm to the touch but have not yet started to brown, 15 to 17 minutes. Remove the sheet from the oven and set it on a wire rack. Let cool for 5 minutes, then use a metal spatula to move the cookies directly to the rack. Let cool completely.

Turn half of the cookies bottom side up and spoon about 1 to 2 teaspoons of the chocolate glaze onto each, almost touching the edges. Top with the remaining cookies, bottom side down. Refrigerate until the filling is firm, about 1 hour. Serve chilled or at room temperature.

Cinnamon-Sugar Roll-Ups

These pretty sweets are just like cinnamon buns in cookie form. To make chocolate-filled roll-ups, use ⅓ cup semisweet chocolate chips, melted, in place of the cinnamon-sugar filling in each rectangle. Spread evenly over the dough, then roll and bake as directed.

MAKES 24 ROLL-UPS

DOUGH

½ cup (1 stick) unsalted butter, at room temperature

4 ounces cream cheese, at room temperature

¼ cup heavy cream

1⅔ cups all-purpose flour

¼ teaspoon salt

FILLING

2½ teaspoons ground cinnamon

½ cup sugar

3 tablespoons unsalted butter, at room temperature

EGG WASH

1 large egg beaten with 1 teaspoon warm water

To make the dough, in a food processor, combine the butter, cream cheese, and cream and process until smooth, about 2 minutes. Add the flour and salt and process until the dough starts to come together, about 1 minute. Dust a clean work surface with flour, then empty the dough onto the surface. Knead the dough a few times, then divide it in half. Form each half into a rectangle, wrap in plastic wrap, and refrigerate for 30 minutes.

Preheat the oven to 375°F. Line 2 cookie sheets with parchment paper.

Set 1 piece of dough on a clean work surface dusted with flour. Roll the dough into a rectangle about 7 by 20 inches, with a long side facing you.

To make the filling, in a small bowl, stir together the cinnamon and sugar. Using your fingers, spread 1½ tablespoons of the butter over the dough, leaving a ½-inch border at the top. Sprinkle half of the cinnamon-sugar mixture over the butter. Starting at the edge closest to you, roll up the dough into a tight log. Press to seal the seam. Using a knife, trim off and discard the ends of the log, then cut the log crosswise into 12 equal slices, each about 1¼ inches thick. Place the slices on 1 of the prepared cookie sheets, turning them cut side up. Repeat with the remaining dough and filling ingredients.

Lightly brush the slices with the egg wash. Bake 1 cookie sheet at a time until the roll-ups are golden brown, about 20 minutes. Remove the sheet from the oven and let cool for 5 minutes on a wire rack, then move the roll-ups directly to the rack. Repeat to bake the remaining roll-ups.

Fortune Cookies

No need to order takeout to enjoy these fun cookies—you can bake your own! Be creative with the messages you write, which is one of the best parts of the process.

MAKES 12 COOKIES

¼ cup all-purpose flour

¼ cup sugar

Pinch of salt

1 large egg white

¼ teaspoon vanilla extract

 Preheat the oven to 375˚F. Line a cookie sheet with parchment paper, then lightly grease the parchment with nonstick cooking spray.

Cut 12 strips of colored or white paper, each about 4 inches long by ½ inch wide. Write a "fortune" on each strip.

In a medium bowl, whisk together the flour, sugar, and salt. In a small bowl, whisk the egg white and vanilla until light and frothy, about 3 minutes. Add the egg white mixture to the flour mixture and stir with a wooden spoon until well combined. The batter will be thin.

Have ready a liquid measuring cup or mug and a muffin pan for shaping the cookies after baking. Scoop 1 teaspoon of the batter onto a prepared cookie sheet and, using a small icing spatula, spread it evenly into a circle about 3 inches in diameter. Repeat to create 3 more circles. Bake until the edges of the cookies are just starting to turn light brown but the centers are still pale, about 5 minutes. Remove the sheet from the oven and, using a metal spatula, move the cookies to a wire rack, turning them upside down. Working quickly, place a fortune in the center of each cookie. Wearing an oven mitt, fold the hot cookies in half and pinch the edges closed. Press the straight edge of a cookie against the rim of the measuring cup and fold it over the rim to create a center crease. Place the cookie in the muffin pan so it keeps its shape. Repeat with the remaining folded cookies. Bake the remaining batter in 2 more batches and shape the cookies in the same way.

Chocolate-Covered Peanut Butter Squares

Crisp peanut butter cookies coated in a rich dark-chocolate glaze—these irresistible treats are like a candy bar and cookie rolled into one. For Halloween treats, decorate them with chocolate, orange, and white sprinkles.

MAKES ABOUT 35 COOKIES

1½ cups all-purpose flour

½ teaspoon baking powder

½ teaspoon baking soda

½ teaspoon salt

½ cup (1 stick) unsalted butter, at room temperature

½ cup firmly packed light brown sugar

½ cup granulated sugar

1 large egg

½ teaspoon vanilla extract

1 cup creamy peanut butter

Chocolate Glaze (see opposite page)

Chocolate, orange, and white sprinkles (optional)

In a medium bowl, whisk together the flour, baking powder, baking soda, and salt. In a large bowl, using an electric mixer, beat the butter, brown sugar, and granulated sugar on medium-high speed until light and fluffy, 2 to 3 minutes. Add the egg and vanilla and beat on low speed until well blended. Add the peanut butter and beat just until well combined. Turn off the mixer and scrape down the bowl with a rubber spatula. Add the flour mixture and mix on low speed just until blended.

Lightly dust a clean work surface with flour. Using the rubber spatula, scrape the dough out onto the work surface. Flour your hands, then form the dough into a flattened rectangle, wrap it tightly in plastic wrap, and refrigerate until firm, at least 1 hour or up to overnight.

Preheat the oven to 350°F. Line 2 cookie sheets with parchment paper.

Lightly dust your work surface with flour, unwrap the dough, and set it on the surface. If the dough is too hard to roll directly from the refrigerator, let it stand at room temperature for a few minutes. Dust your rolling pin with flour and roll out the dough to a 15-by-11-inch rectangle about ¼ inch thick. Using a pizza wheel or sharp paring knife, trim the edges of the rectangle so that it measures 14 by 10 inches. Cut out thirty-five 2-inch squares. With a metal spatula, carefully move the squares to the prepared cookie sheets, spacing them 1 inch apart.

PB-palooza

Add a thin layer of peanut butter on top of the cookies and chill for 10 minutes before you dip them in chocolate.

Bake 1 cookie sheet at a time until the edges of the cookies are light brown, 15 to 18 minutes. Remove the sheet from the oven and set it on a wire rack. Let cool for 5 minutes then move the cookies directly to the wire rack. Repeat to bake the rest of the cookies. Let cool completely. Reserve the parchment-lined cookie sheets.

Dip each cookie into the chocolate glaze and use 2 forks to turn the cookie so that it's coated on both sides. Using the forks, lift out the cookie and gently shake it, allowing excess glaze to fall back into the bowl. Place the glazed cookie on 1 of the parchment-lined cookie sheets. Repeat with the remaining cookies and glaze. Decorate with sprinkles, if using. Refrigerate the cookies uncovered until the glaze is set, about 30 minutes. Serve the cookies chilled.

Chocolate Glaze

In a small saucepan, combine ½ cup heavy cream and 1½ tablespoons room-temperature unsalted butter. Set the pan over medium-high heat and bring the mixture to a boil. Remove from the heat. Add 6 ounces finely chopped semisweet chocolate and a pinch of salt and carefully swirl the pan to cover the chocolate with cream. Let stand for 1 minute, then slowly whisk the mixture until smooth. Transfer to a small bowl and let cool, stirring frequently, until the glaze is thick enough to coat the back of a spoon, 40 to 45 minutes. (If the glaze becomes too thick, place it in a microwave-safe bowl and microwave on high power, stirring every 15 seconds, until it reaches the right consistency.)

Gingersnap Snowflakes

Crisp and full of flavor, gingersnaps are a delicious holiday tradition, filling your kitchen with wonderful aromas. They're perfect for gifting because they stay snappy for days and are easy to pack in decorative boxes or cellophane bags tied with pretty ribbon.

MAKES ABOUT 48 COOKIES

6 cups all-purpose flour

1 tablespoon baking soda

1 cup (2 sticks)
unsalted butter,
at room temperature

2½ cups granulated sugar

¾ cup dark corn syrup

¾ cup water

1 tablespoon
ground cinnamon

1 tablespoon
ground cloves

1 tablespoon
ground ginger

Vanilla Icing (page 36)

White sanding sugar,
for decorating (optional)

 Preheat the oven to 350°F. Line 2 cookie sheets with parchment paper.

In a large bowl, whisk together the flour and baking soda. In another large bowl, using an electric mixer, beat the butter and granulated sugar on medium speed until light and fluffy, about 3 minutes. Set aside.

In a medium saucepan, combine the corn syrup, water, and spices. Set the pan over medium-high heat and bring the mixture to a boil, stirring occasionally. Turn off the heat and let cool for 5 minutes. Pour the mixture into the butter-sugar mixture and stir until combined. Gradually stir in the flour mixture, mixing just until combined. Using floured hands, form the dough into a rectangle, wrap it tightly in plastic wrap, and refrigerate until firm, about 2 hours.

Dust your work surface with flour and set the dough on it. Cut it into 4 pieces. Roll out 1 piece of dough to ¼-inch thickness. Using snowflake cookie cutters, cut out shapes from the dough. Transfer the cutouts to the prepared cookie sheets, spacing them about 1 inch apart. Repeat with the remaining pieces of dough and any dough scraps.

Bake 1 cookie sheet at a time until the cookies are firm to the touch, 10 to 12 minutes. Remove the sheet from the oven and let cool for 5 minutes on a wire rack, then move the cookies to the rack. Repeat to bake the remaining cookies.

Decorate the cookies with vanilla icing and sanding sugar as desired. Let the icing dry at room temperature until firm, at least 2 hours or up to overnight.

Milk-and-Cookie Cups

Cookies and milk are a perfect pairing, so why not combine them into mini chocolate chip cookie cups coated with chocolate, then filled with cold milk? Make these sweets for a sleepover and watch the reactions when you pour milk right into the cookies!

MAKES 36 COOKIE CUPS

2 cups all-purpose flour

½ teaspoon salt

1 cup (2 sticks) unsalted butter, at room temperature

½ cup firmly packed light brown sugar

½ cup granulated sugar

1 large egg

2 teaspoons vanilla extract

1 (12-ounce) bag mini semisweet chocolate chips

1½ cups cold whole milk, for serving

Grease a 24-cup mini muffin pan with nonstick cooking spray.

In a medium bowl, whisk together the flour and salt. In a large bowl, using an electric mixer, beat the butter, brown sugar, and granulated sugar on medium speed until well blended, about 1 minute. Add the egg and vanilla and beat on low speed until well combined. Turn off the mixer and scrape down the bowl with a rubber spatula. Add about half of the flour mixture and mix on low speed just until blended. Add the rest of the flour mixture and mix again just until blended. Turn off the mixer, add ¾ cup of the chocolate chips, and stir with a wooden spoon until the chips are mixed evenly into the dough.

Spoon 1 tablespoon of dough into each muffin cup, pushing the dough into the bottom and up the sides of each cup so that the dough rises slightly above the rim. Use a ½-teaspoon measuring spoon to smooth the center well. Refrigerate the pan, uncovered, for 30 minutes. Cover the bowl containing the remaining dough with plastic wrap and refrigerate while the first batch chills and bakes.

~ Continued on page 94 ~

Handy measures

Use a ½-teaspoon measuring spoon to shape the cookie cups before and after they're baked.

~ *Continued from page 93* ~

Preheat the oven to 350°F.

Bake the cookie cups until the edges begin to brown, about 20 minutes. Remove the pan from the oven and set it on a wire rack. Immediately use the ½-teaspoon measuring spoon to smooth the center wells once again. Let cool for 15 minutes, then carefully remove the cookie cups, using a small icing spatula to help loosen them, and set them directly on the rack. Let the muffin pan cool completely. Remove the remaining dough from the refrigerator and bake the second batch in the same way. Let the cookie cups cool completely.

Add the remaining chocolate chips to a medium microwave-safe bowl. Microwave on high power, stirring every 15 seconds, just until the chips are melted and smooth. Don't let the chocolate get too hot!

Spoon about ½ teaspoon of the melted chocolate into each cookie cup. Tip and rotate the cups so that the chocolate coats the sides. Let the chocolate set for 20 minutes.

Just before serving, fill each cookie cup with milk.

Lemon-Lime Thumbprint Cookies

These treats get their name from the little indentations pressed into the centers of the cookies—they look like they were formed with a tip of the thumb. The centers are usually filled with jam or fruit preserves, but these contain homemade lemon curd.

MAKES ABOUT 24 COOKIES

COOKIES

2 cups all-purpose flour

½ teaspoon salt

1 cup (2 sticks)
unsalted butter,
at room temperature

½ cup granulated sugar

2 teaspoons
vanilla extract

LEMON CURD

2 lemons

4 large egg yolks

⅔ cup granulated sugar

Pinch of salt

5 tablespoons unsalted
butter, cut into 5 pieces

LEMON GLAZE

1 cup powdered sugar

2 tablespoons fresh
lime or lemon juice

 To make the cookies, in a medium bowl, whisk together the flour and salt. In a large bowl, using an electric mixer, beat the butter and granulated sugar on medium speed until light and fluffy, about 3 minutes. Add the vanilla and beat on low speed until combined, about 1 minute. Turn off the mixer and scrape down the bowl with a rubber spatula. Add the flour mixture and beat on low speed just until blended.

Lightly dust a clean work surface with flour. Using the rubber spatula, scrape the dough onto the surface, then use your hands to shape the dough into a disk. Wrap the disk in plastic wrap and refrigerate for 30 minutes.

Meanwhile, make the lemon curd. Finely grate the zest from the lemons. Cut the lemons in half and squeeze enough juice to measure ⅓ cup. In a heavy-bottomed medium saucepan, whisk together the egg yolks, lemon zest and juice, granulated sugar, and salt. Set the pan over medium-high heat and cook, whisking constantly and scraping the corners of the pan, until the mixture is thick enough to coat the back of a spoon, 5 to 8 minutes; do not let the curd boil, or it will turn lumpy. Immediately remove the pan from the heat and whisk in the butter, one piece at a time, until the curd is smooth. Set a fine-mesh sieve over a medium bowl. Pour the curd into the sieve and stir it to help it pass through. Cover the bowl with plastic wrap.

~ *Continued on page 100* ~

Lemon shortcut

Instead of making your own lemon curd, buy a jar from the grocery store. You'll need about 1 cup.

~ *Continued from page 99* ~

Preheat the oven to 350°F. Line 2 cookie sheets with parchment paper.

Remove the dough from the refrigerator. Scoop up 1 heaping teaspoon of dough. Scrape the dough off the spoon into your palms and roll the dough into a ball. Place the ball on a prepared cookie sheet. Continue scooping and rolling the dough, spacing the balls about 2 inches apart on the cookie sheets. You should be able to fit 12 cookies on each sheet. Press each ball with the palm of your hand to flatten it slightly. Use the back of a 1-teaspoon measuring spoon, or your thumb, to make an indentation in the center of each cookie. If the dough forms cracks around the edges, patch them by smoothing the crack together gently with your fingers.

Bake 1 cookie sheet until the dough has just started to set, about 8 minutes. Remove the sheet from the oven and set it on a wire rack. If the indentations have filled in, carefully press the back of the 1-teaspoon measuring spoon into the center of the hot cookies. Spoon ¼ teaspoon lemon curd into each indentation, then carefully return the cookie sheet to the oven. Bake until the curd is set, about 5 minutes more. (Be careful not to overbake or the curd will start to get runny and spread over the edges.) Remove the sheet from the oven and return it to the rack. Let cool for 5 minutes, then move the cookies directly to the rack. Repeat to bake and fill the rest of the cookies. Let cool completely.

To make the glaze, in a small bowl, whisk the powdered sugar and lime juice until smooth. Using a spoon, drizzle the glaze over the cooled cookies. Let the glaze dry for about 15 minutes and serve.

Glazed Lemon-Buttermilk Icebox Cookies

Pucker up! Lemon zest and juice give these slice-and-bake cookies lots of lemony flavor, and buttermilk makes their texture soft and cakelike. They're perfect for a tea party. You can add 1 to 2 dabs of yellow gel paste food coloring to the lemon glaze.

MAKES ABOUT 48 COOKIES

COOKIES

2 cups all-purpose flour

¾ teaspoon baking soda

½ teaspoon salt

¾ cup (1½ sticks) unsalted butter, at room temperature

1 cup granulated sugar

1 large egg

2 tablespoons finely grated lemon zest

3 tablespoons buttermilk

1 teaspoon fresh lemon juice

Lemon Glaze (see page 99), doubled

Colored sanding sugar, edible beads, and/or candy flowers, for decorating (optional)

In a medium bowl, whisk together the flour, baking soda, and salt. In a large bowl, using an electric mixer, beat the butter and granulated sugar on medium-high speed until light and fluffy, 2 to 3 minutes. Add the egg and lemon zest and beat on low speed until combined. Add the flour mixture and mix on low speed just until blended. Add the buttermilk and lemon juice and beat just until combined.

Lightly dust a clean work surface with flour and set the dough on the surface. With your hands, shape the dough into an even log about 12 inches long. Wrap the log tightly in plastic wrap and refrigerate until firm, at least 3 hours or up to overnight.

Preheat the oven to 350°F. Line 2 cookie sheets with parchment paper.

Unwrap the log and set it on a cutting board. Cut the log into slices about ¼ inch thick; discard the ends. Place the slices on the prepared cookie sheets, spacing them about 1 inch apart. Bake 1 cookie sheet at a time until the edges of the cookies are light golden brown, about 12 minutes. Remove the sheet from the oven and set it on a wire rack. Let cool for 5 minutes, then move the cookies directly to the rack. Let cool completely. Repeat to bake the rest of the cookies.

Using a small icing spatula, spread the glaze onto the cookies. Sprinkle with sanding sugar or other decorations, if using. Let the glaze dry for about 1 hour.

Brownies
& Bars

Share the love
Wrap individual bars in a piece of colored paper and tie with twine for a super cute homemade gift.

Ooey-Gooey Layer Bars

You don't even need a mixing bowl to make these buttery, nutty, chocolaty bars!
Just layer the ingredients in the baking pan and pop the whole thing in the oven.
If you like, you can swap the butterscotch chips for peanut butter chips.

MAKES 20 BARS

**10 graham crackers,
broken into pieces**

**½ cup (1 stick)
unsalted butter,
melted**

**1½ cups semisweet
chocolate chips**

1 cup butterscotch chips

**1 cup old-fashioned
rolled oats**

**1 cup pecans, toasted
and chopped (optional)**

**1 cup walnuts, toasted
and chopped (optional)**

**1 (14-ounce) can
sweetened condensed milk**

**1½ cups shredded dried
unsweetened coconut**

Preheat the oven to 350°F. Put the graham cracker pieces in a
zipper-lock plastic bag. Press out the air and seal the bag. Use a
rolling pin to crush the crackers into fine crumbs, pounding them lightly
or using a gentle back-and-forth rolling motion. You should have about
1½ cups of crumbs.

Pour the butter into a 9-by-13-inch baking pan and carefully tilt the pan
to coat the sides. Sprinkle the graham cracker crumbs in an even layer in
the pan. Layer in the chocolate chips, butterscotch chips, oats, and, if using,
the pecans and walnuts. Pour the condensed milk evenly over the top,
then sprinkle with the coconut. Bake until the coconut is golden brown,
20 to 25 minutes. Remove the pan from the oven and set it on a wire rack.
Let cool completely.

Cut the bar into 20 rectangles and serve.

Sugar Cookie Bars

This bar-shaped sugar cookie is super chewy, thanks to the cream cheese in the dough. And, topped with fluffy pink frosting and colorful sprinkles, it's also super pretty! Instead of rainbow sprinkles, you can use confetti, heart-shaped, or star-shaped sprinkles.

MAKES 20 BARS

SUGAR COOKIE

2¾ cups all-purpose flour

½ teaspoon salt

1 cup (2 sticks) unsalted butter, at room temperature

1 (8-ounce) package cream cheese, at room temperature

1½ cups granulated sugar

1 large egg

2 teaspoons vanilla extract

FROSTING

¾ cup (1½ sticks) unsalted butter, at room temperature

4 cups powdered sugar

2 teaspoons vanilla extract

¼ cup fresh blood orange juice or ¼ cup whole milk, plus a few dabs of red gel paste food coloring

Salt

Rainbow sprinkles, for decorating

 Preheat the oven to 350°F. Lightly butter a 9-by-13-inch baking pan. Line the pan with parchment paper, running it up the two long sides of the pan and letting it extend past the rim by about 2 inches. Butter the parchment.

To make the sugar cookie, in a medium bowl, whisk together the flour and salt. In a large bowl, using an electric mixer, beat the butter and cream cheese on medium speed until well blended, about 1 minute. Add the granulated sugar and beat until smooth. Add the egg and vanilla and beat on low speed until well combined. Turn off the mixer and scrape down the bowl with a rubber spatula. Add the flour mixture and mix on low speed just until blended.

Scrape the dough into the prepared baking pan and press it into an even layer with the spatula. Bake until the edges are light brown, about 30 minutes. Remove the pan from the oven and set it on a wire rack. Let cool completely.

To make the frosting, place the butter in a large bowl. Using an electric mixer, beat the butter on medium speed until creamy, about 1 minute. Add the powdered sugar 1 cup at a time, beating on low speed until combined after each addition. Add the vanilla, blood orange juice, and a pinch of salt and beat on medium speed until the frosting is light and fluffy.

Holding the ends of the parchment paper like handles, lift the cookie out of the pan and set it on a cutting board. Using a spatula, spread the frosting on top, then decorate with rainbow sprinkles. Cut it into 20 bars and serve.

Chocolate Chip Blondies

Do you love both chewy chocolate chip cookies and rich, moist brownies? Then these yummy treats are just for you. You can swap out the semisweet chocolate chips for butterscotch, peanut butter, milk chocolate, or white chocolate—or use a mix.

MAKES 24 BARS

2¾ cups all-purpose flour

2½ teaspoons baking powder

¼ teaspoon salt

¾ cup (1½ sticks) unsalted butter, at room temperature

2⅓ cups firmly packed dark brown sugar

3 large eggs

2 teaspoons vanilla extract

2 cups semisweet chocolate chips, plus ⅓ cup for drizzling

 Preheat the oven to 350°F. Butter a 9-by-13-inch baking pan.

In a medium bowl, whisk together the flour, baking powder, and salt. In a large bowl, using an electric mixer, beat the butter and brown sugar on medium speed until light and fluffy, 3 to 5 minutes. Add the eggs one at a time, beating well after each addition. Add the vanilla and beat until well combined. Turn off the mixer and scrape down the bowl with a rubber spatula. Add about half of the flour mixture and mix on low speed just until blended. Add the remaining flour mixture and mix again just until blended. Turn off the mixer, add the 2 cups of chocolate chips and stir with a wooden spoon until the chips are mixed evenly into the batter.

Using the rubber spatula, scrape the batter into the prepared pan and smooth the top. Bake until the top is golden brown, 40 to 45 minutes. Remove the pan from the oven and set it on a wire rack. Let the blondies cool completely in the pan.

Place the remaining ⅓ cup chocolate chips in a small microwave-safe bowl. Microwave on high power, stirring every 20 seconds, just until the chips are melted and smooth. Don't let the chocolate get too hot! Cut the blondies, still in the pan, into 24 bars. Using a fork, drizzle the melted chocolate over the bars. Let stand until the chocolate sets, about 30 minutes, then serve.

Mini Coconut-Lemon Squares

Classic lemon bars get an upgrade with chewy shredded coconut. Be sure to use sweetened coconut here, not the unsweetened type, or the bars might make your lips pucker! Remember that it's easier to zest the lemon before you juice it.

MAKES 48 BARS

CRUST

1½ cups all-purpose flour

½ cup powdered sugar

1½ teaspoons finely grated lemon zest

⅛ teaspoon salt

¾ cup (1½ sticks) cold unsalted butter, cut into ½-inch pieces

FILLING

½ cup all-purpose flour

2½ cups granulated sugar

6 large eggs

1 tablespoon finely grated lemon zest

¾ cup fresh lemon juice

2 cups sweetened shredded coconut

 Preheat the oven to 325°F. Lightly butter a 9-by-13-inch baking pan. Line the pan with parchment paper, running it up the two long sides of the pan and letting it extend past the rim by about 2 inches. Butter the parchment.

To make the crust, in a large bowl, combine the flour, powdered sugar, zest, and salt. Using an electric mixer, mix on low speed just to blend the ingredients, about 1 minute. Turn off the mixer and add the butter. Beat on low speed until the butter is in pieces no larger than the size of peas, about 2 minutes. Scrape the dough into the prepared baking pan. Using a rubber spatula, firmly and evenly press the dough into the bottom of the pan. Bake just until the edges of the crust are lightly browned, about 20 minutes. Remove the pan from the oven and set it on a wire rack. Reduce the oven temperature to 300°F.

To make the filling, in a large bowl, whisk together the flour and granulated sugar. Add the eggs and lemon zest and juice and whisk until well blended, about 1 minute. Add the coconut and stir until well mixed. Slowly pour the filling into the crust. Bake until the filling does not wobble when the pan is gently shaken, 40 to 45 minutes. Remove the pan from the oven and return it to the rack. Let cool for about 1 hour. Cover the pan with plastic wrap and refrigerate until the filling is firm, about 4 hours.

Holding the ends of the parchment paper like handles, lift the bar out of the pan and set it on a cutting board. Cut it into 48 squares and serve. (Store the bars in an airtight container in the refrigerator for up to 2 days.)

Crispy Rice and Chocolate Layer Brownies

Crispy, chewy, peanut buttery, and oh-so chocolaty, these eye-catching
bar cookies are sure to be crowd-pleasers. The trick to easy assembly is
making sure that each layer is completely cooled before adding the next one.

MAKES 16 BROWNIES

BROWNIES

½ cup (1 stick) unsalted
butter, cut into 4 pieces

3 ounces unsweetened
chocolate, finely chopped

1 cup sugar

Pinch of salt

2 large eggs

1 teaspoon vanilla extract

¾ cup all-purpose flour

¾ cup bittersweet
chocolate chips

CHOCOLATE LAYER

1⅓ cups semisweet or
bittersweet chocolate chips

1 cup heavy cream

Pinch of salt

Preheat the oven to 325°F. Butter an 8-inch square baking pan. Line
the pan with parchment paper, letting it extend past the rim on two
sides by about 2 inches. Butter the parchment.

To make the brownies, in a large microwave-safe bowl, combine the butter
and chocolate. Microwave on high power, stirring every 30 seconds, just
until the mixture is melted and smooth. Don't let it get too hot! Add the sugar
and salt and whisk until blended. Add the eggs and vanilla and whisk until
well combined. Add the flour and bittersweet chocolate chips and stir with
a wooden spoon just until there are no white streaks in the batter and the
chips are evenly mixed in.

Pour the batter into the prepared pan and use a rubber spatula to spread
evenly. Bake until a toothpick inserted into the center of the brownies comes
out with a few moist crumbs attached, about 30 minutes. Remove the pan
from the oven and set it on a wire rack. Let cool to room temperature.

To make the chocolate layer, put the semisweet chocolate chips in a heatproof
medium bowl. Pour the cream into a small saucepan and bring it to a boil over
medium-high heat. Immediately pour the cream over the chocolate chips and
add the salt. Let stand for 10 minutes, then whisk until smooth and shiny.
Refrigerate until the mixture is chilled but not hardened, about 20 minutes.

~ Continued on page 112 ~

Try this!

To cut gooey bars and treats with less mess, dip your knife into a glass of hot water before you use it.

~ Continued from page 111 ~

Measure out ¼ cup of the chocolate mixture and set aside. Pour the remaining chocolate mixture onto the brownies and spread it evenly with a spatula. Place the pan in the refrigerator.

To make the peanut butter crispy rice, in a large saucepan, melt the butter over low heat. Add the marshmallows and stir with a wooden spoon until melted. Remove the pan from the heat, add the peanut butter, and stir until fully blended. Add the rice cereal and stir until evenly coated. Let cool completely.

Scoop the peanut butter–rice cereal mixture on top of the chocolate layer. Using a rubber spatula, gently press it into an even layer. Using a spoon, drizzle the reserved chocolate mixture on top. Let cool.

Holding the ends of the parchment paper like handles, lift the bar out of the pan and set it on a cutting board. Cut it into 16 squares and serve.

PEANUT BUTTER CRISPY RICE

5 tablespoons unsalted butter

5 cups mini marshmallows

½ cup creamy peanut butter

5 cups crispy rice cereal

Mini Cheesecake Bars

You don't need a fork to eat cheesecake! These rich and creamy,
easy-to-make bars are finger food, so they're perfect
for a tea party or summer picnic.

MAKES 48 BARS

CRUST

20 graham crackers, broken into pieces

2 tablespoons sugar

¾ teaspoon ground cinnamon

½ cup (1 stick) unsalted butter, melted

FILLING

3 (8-ounce) packages cream cheese, at room temperature

1 cup sugar

2 teaspoons vanilla extract

1 teaspoon ground cinnamon

3 tablespoons all-purpose flour

4 large eggs, at room temperature

½ cup sour cream

 Preheat the oven to 325°F. Lightly butter a 9-by-13-inch baking pan. Line the pan with parchment paper, running it up the two long sides of the pan and letting it extend past the rim by about 2 inches. Butter the parchment.

To make the crust, put the graham cracker pieces in a zipper-lock plastic bag. Press out the air and seal the bag. Use a rolling pin to crush the crackers into fine crumbs. You should have about 3 cups. Empty the crumbs into a medium bowl and stir in the sugar, cinnamon, and melted butter until the crumbs are moistened. Pour the crumbs into the prepared pan and press into an even layer in the bottom of the pan. Bake until the crust darkens slightly, about 10 minutes. Remove the pan from the oven and set it on a wire rack.

To make the filling, in a large bowl, using an electric mixer, beat the cream cheese, sugar, vanilla, and cinnamon on medium speed until well blended, about 1 minute. Add the flour and beat on low speed just until blended, about 1 minute. Add the eggs one at a time, beating well after each addition. Add the sour cream and beat just until combined, about 30 seconds. Pour the filling into the crust. Bake until the filling does not wobble when the pan is gently shaken, 40 to 45 minutes. Remove from the oven and set on a wire rack. Let cool for about 1 hour. Cover with plastic wrap and refrigerate until the filling is firm, about 4 hours.

Holding the ends of the parchment paper like handles, lift the bar out of the pan and set it on a cutting board. Cut it into 48 bars and serve.

Frosted Chocolate Brownies

Just in case you can't get enough chocolate, these gooey brownies are topped with a fluffy chocolate frosting. If you're packing these treats to go, skip the frosting because it will get smooshed—or bring it with you in a separate container.

MAKES 16 BROWNIES

BROWNIES

¾ cup (1½ sticks) unsalted butter, at room temperature

5 ounces unsweetened chocolate, chopped

1 cup all-purpose flour

¼ teaspoon salt

4 large eggs

2 cups granulated sugar

1 teaspoon vanilla extract

FROSTING

2 ounces bittersweet chocolate, chopped

½ cup (1 stick) unsalted butter, at room temperature

1 cup powdered sugar

1 teaspoon vanilla extract

1 tablespoon heavy cream

 Preheat the oven to 325°F. Lightly butter a 9-by-13-inch baking pan. Line the pan with parchment paper, running it up the two long sides of the pan and letting it extend past the rim by about 2 inches. Butter the parchment.

To make the brownies, in a large microwave-safe bowl, combine the butter and chocolate. Microwave on high power, stirring every 30 seconds, just until the mixture is melted and smooth. Don't let it get too hot! Set aside to cool slightly.

In a small bowl, whisk together the flour and salt; set aside. Add the eggs to the warm chocolate mixture and whisk until well blended. Add the sugar and vanilla and whisk until well combined. Add the flour mixture and whisk just until there are no white streaks in the batter. Pour into the prepared pan and bake until a toothpick inserted in the center comes out with moist crumbs, 30 to 35 minutes. Remove from the oven and let cool completely on a wire rack.

Meanwhile, make the frosting. Melt the chocolate as you did for the brownies. Let cool for about 5 minutes. In a large bowl, using an electric mixer, beat the butter and powdered sugar on medium speed until well blended, about 1 minute. Add the vanilla, cream, and melted chocolate and beat on medium speed until the mixture is evenly colored and the frosting is fluffy, about 2 minutes.

Holding the ends of the parchment paper like handles, lift the brownie out of the pan and set it on a cutting board. Using an offset spatula, spread the frosting evenly on the brownie. Carefully cut it into 16 squares and serve.

S'mores Bars

You don't need a campfire to enjoy all the chocolaty, marshmallowy goodness of s'mores. With this recipe, an electric mixer and an oven are all it takes. Have lots of napkins ready because these yummy bars are messy—in a good way!

MAKES 16 BARS

2 cups all-purpose flour

1 teaspoon baking soda

1 teaspoon salt

1 cup (2 sticks) unsalted butter, at room temperature

1 cup firmly packed light brown sugar

½ cup granulated sugar

2 large eggs

2 teaspoons vanilla extract

10 graham crackers, broken into pieces and crushed into crumbs (see page 114)

1 cup semisweet chocolate chips

1½ cups marshmallows

 Preheat the oven to 350°F. Butter an 8-inch square baking pan. Line the pan with parchment paper, letting it extend past the rim on two sides by about 2 inches. Butter the parchment.

In a medium bowl, whisk together the flour, baking soda, and salt. In a large bowl, using an electric mixer, beat the butter and both sugars on medium speed until light and fluffy, about 5 minutes. Add the eggs one at a time, beating well after each addition. Add the vanilla and beat until well combined. Add the flour mixture and mix on low speed just until blended. Add the graham cracker crumbs and mix until well combined.

Place about two-thirds of the dough in the prepared baking pan and press it into an even layer in the bottom of the pan. Sprinkle the chocolate chips evenly over the dough. Layer the marshmallows on top of the chocolate chips so that they are touching, squishing them in so they fit tightly. Pinch off a chunk of the remaining dough and flatten it between your palms until the dough is about ½ inch thick. (If the dough gets too sticky, flour your hands first.) Place the piece on top of the marshmallows. Repeat with the rest of the dough, layering the piece to cover the marshmallows; it's fine if a little bit of marshmallow shows through. Bake until the top is light brown, about 40 minutes. Remove the pan from the oven and let cool completely on a wire rack.

Holding the ends of the parchment paper like handles, lift the bar out of the pan and set it on a cutting board. Carefully cut it into 16 squares and serve.

Raspberry-Oat Streusel Bars

Packed with oats and filled with jam, these crunchy, chewy bars are an awesome snack or dessert—and they make a great breakfast, too. Plus they're easy to pack for lunch or a picnic. You can swap the raspberry jam for strawberry, blueberry, or apricot.

MAKES 20 BARS

1⅔ cups unbleached all-purpose flour

1 cup firmly packed light brown sugar

¾ cup (1½ sticks) cold unsalted butter, cut into 12 even chunks

2 teaspoons vanilla extract

1 teaspoon ground cinnamon

½ teaspoon salt

¼ teaspoon baking soda

Finely grated zest from 1 small orange

1⅔ cups old-fashioned rolled oats

1½ cups raspberry jam

Preheat the oven to 350°F. Generously butter a 9-by-13-inch baking pan.

In a food processor, combine the flour, sugar, butter, vanilla, cinnamon, salt, baking soda, and orange zest. Pulse until the mixture forms coarse crumbs, 10 to 12 quick pulses. Add the oats and pulse until well mixed, just a few more quick pulses.

Transfer about two-thirds of the oat mixture into the prepared pan. Using your hands, firmly press it into an even layer in the bottom of the pan. Using a spatula, spread the jam evenly on the top. Sprinkle the remaining oat mixture evenly on top of the jam. Bake until the top is golden brown and the jam is bubbling, 35 to 40 minutes. Remove the pan from the oven and set it on a wire rack. Let cool completely.

Cut it into 20 rectangles and serve.

Sprechen sie Deutsch?

Streusel (pronounced STROO-sul) is a German word that refers to a crumbly mixture of flour, butter, and sugar.

Cream Cheese Swirl Brownies

Can't decide between cheesecake and brownies? With this combo, you can have both!
You can swap the cream cheese for other mix-ins. Swirl in ¾ cup of raspberry jam or
peanut butter in place of the cream cheese batter and bake for 30 to 35 minutes instead.

MAKES 16 BROWNIES

BROWNIE BATTER

**½ cup (1 stick)
unsalted butter**,
at room temperature

**4 ounces unsweetened
chocolate, finely chopped**

1 cup all-purpose flour

¼ teaspoon salt

3 large eggs

1¾ cups sugar

1 teaspoon vanilla extract

CREAM CHEESE BATTER

6 ounces cream cheese,
at room temperature

¼ cup sugar

1 large egg

1 teaspoon vanilla extract

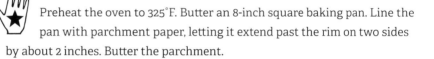

Preheat the oven to 325°F. Butter an 8-inch square baking pan. Line the pan with parchment paper, letting it extend past the rim on two sides by about 2 inches. Butter the parchment.

To make the brownie batter, in a medium microwave-safe bowl, combine the butter and chocolate. Microwave on high power, stirring every 30 seconds, just until the mixture is melted and smooth. Set aside to cool slightly.

In a small bowl, whisk together the flour and salt; set aside. Add the eggs to the warm chocolate mixture and whisk until well blended. Add the sugar and vanilla and whisk until well combined. Add the flour mixture and whisk just until there are no white streaks in the batter. Set the batter aside.

To make the cream cheese batter, in another medium bowl, combine the cream cheese, sugar, egg, and vanilla. Using an electric mixer, beat on medium speed until well blended, about 4 minutes.

Pour two-thirds of the brownie batter into the prepared pan, then spoon in the cream cheese batter. Pour the remaining brownie batter on top and swirl a spoon through the mixture to create a marbled look. Bake until a toothpick inserted in the center comes out with a few moist crumbs, 35 to 40 minutes. Remove the pan from the oven and let cool completely on a wire rack. Once the brownie is cool, hold the ends of the parchment paper like handles, lift the brownie out of the pan, and set it on a cutting board. Cut it into 16 squares.

Millionaire's Shortbread

No one knows for sure how these bar cookies got their name, but one thing's certain: they are super rich—like a millionaire! Buttery shortbread is topped with a layer of creamy caramel and finished with a coating of dark chocolate.

MAKES 16 BARS

SHORTBREAD

1½ cups all-purpose flour

½ teaspoon salt

1 cup (2 sticks)
unsalted butter,
at room temperature

¼ cup firmly packed
light brown sugar

¼ cup granulated sugar

1 large egg yolk

1 teaspoon vanilla extract

CARAMEL

¾ cup (1½ sticks)
unsalted butter,
at room temperature

¾ cup firmly packed
dark brown sugar

1 (14-ounce) can
sweetened condensed milk

Pinch of salt

8 ounces semisweet
chocolate, chopped

Flaky sea salt,
for sprinkling

Preheat the oven to 300°F. Butter a 9-inch square baking pan. Line the pan with parchment paper, letting it extend past the rim on two sides by about 2 inches. Butter the parchment.

To make the shortbread, in a small bowl, whisk together the flour and salt. In a large bowl, using an electric mixer, beat the butter on high speed until light and fluffy, about 3 minutes. Add both sugars and beat until well blended, about 3 minutes. Add the egg yolk and vanilla and beat until combined. Add the flour mixture and mix on low speed just until blended. Using floured fingertips, press the dough into an even layer in the bottom of the pan. Bake until the edges are light golden brown, about 45 minutes. Remove the pan from the oven and let cool completely on a wire rack.

To make the caramel, combine the butter and sugar in a medium saucepan. Set the pan over medium-low heat and cook, stirring occasionally, until the butter and sugar are melted. Add the condensed milk and salt and bring to a boil, stirring constantly; boil for 1 minute longer. Remove the pan from the heat and carefully pour the caramel over the shortbread. Let cool for 10 minutes, then refrigerate until the caramel is firm and set, about 30 minutes.

Place the chocolate in a small microwave-safe bowl. Microwave on high power, stirring every 30 seconds, until the chocolate is melted. Pour over the caramel, then lightly sprinkle with flaky sea salt. Refrigerate until the chocolate has set, about 15 minutes. Lift the bar out of the pan, cut it into 16 squares, and serve.

Salty sweet

If you're a fan of salted caramel, stir 1 teaspoon salt into the caramel after you remove it from the heat, and skip the salt sprinkles at the end.

Index

Weldon Owen is a division of Bonnier Publishing USA

1045 Sansome Street, Suite 100, San Francisco, CA 94111
www.weldonowen.com

WELDON OWEN, INC.
President & Publisher Roger Shaw
SVP, Sales & Marketing Amy Kaneko

Associate Publisher Amy Marr
Project Editor Alexis Mersel

Creative Director Kelly Booth
Associate Art Director Lisa Berman
Original Design Alexandra Zeigler

Production Director Michelle Duggan
Imaging Manager Don Hill

Photographer Nicole Hill Gerulat
Food Stylist Tara Bench
Wardrobe & Prop Stylists Veronica Olson
Hair & Makeup Kathy Hill

AMERICAN GIRL *COOKIES*
Conceived and produced by Weldon Owen, Inc.

A WELDON OWEN PRODUCTION
Copyright © 2018 American Girl
All rights reserved, including the right of
reproduction in whole or in part in any form.
All American Girl marks are owned by and
used under license from American Girl.
Printed and bound in China

First printed in 2018
10 9 8 7 6 5 4 3 2 1

Library of Congress Cataloging in Publication
data is available

ISBN: 978-1-68188-442-4

ACKNOWLEDGMENTS
Weldon Owen wishes to thank the following people for their generous support to help produce this book:
Mary Bench, Lou Bustamante, Laken Flinders, Lindsey Hargett, David Meredith, Taylor Olson

A VERY SPECIAL THANK YOU TO:
Our models: Evie Gerulat, Jane Jensen, Ruby Robinson, Naledi Sefolosha, Lucy Smith, Sylvie Stafford

Our locations: The Gerulat Family

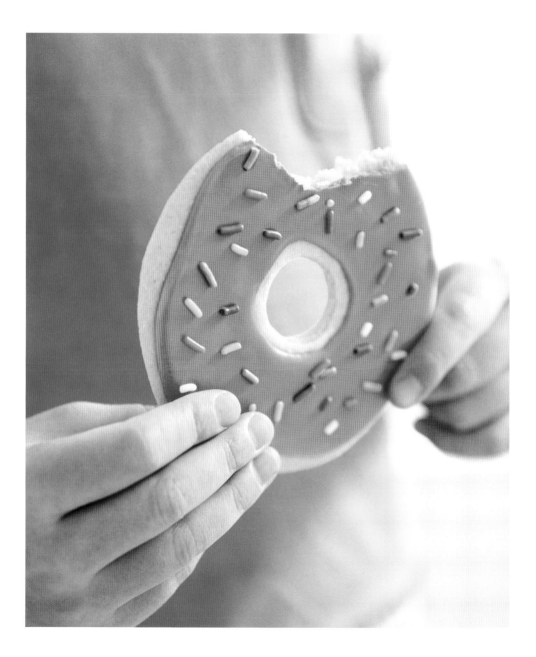

Collect Them All

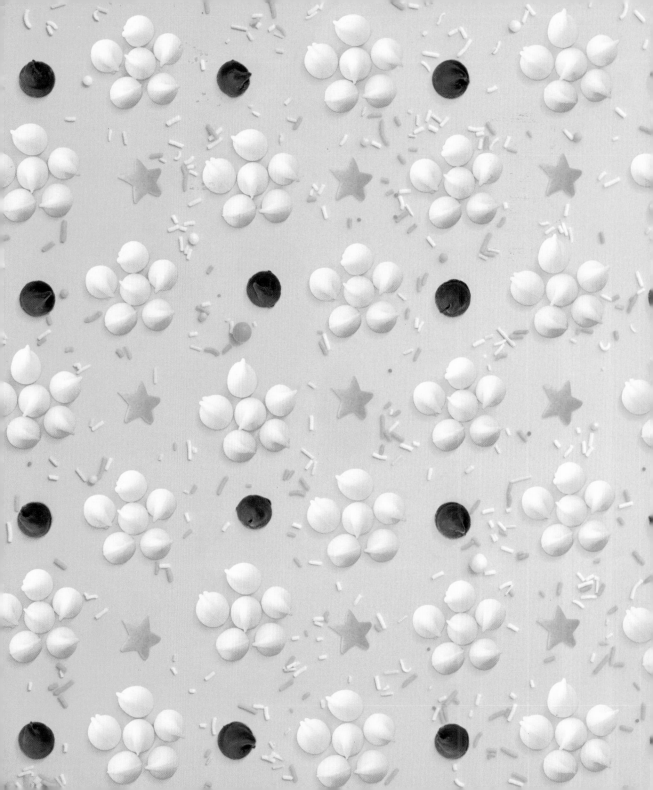